D1606355

THE PASSIONS OF

SHAKESPEARE'S

TRAGIC HEROES

The *Passions* of
Shakespeare's
Tragic Heroes

ARTHUR KIRSCH

University Press of Virginia
Charlottesville and London

20934328

PR
2983
·K497
1990

THE UNIVERSITY PRESS OF VIRGINIA
Copyright © 1990 by the Rector and Visitors
of the University of Virginia

First published 1990

Library of Congress Cataloging-in-Publication Data

Kirsch, Arthur.
    The passions of Shakespeare's tragic heroes / Arthur Kirsch.
      p.   cm.
    Includes bibliographical references.
    ISBN 0-8139-1277-6
    1. Shakespeare, William, 1564–1616—Tragedies. 2. Shapespeare,
William, 1564–1616—Characters—Heroes. 3. Emotions in Literature.
4. Heroes in literature. 5. Tragedy. I. Title.
PR2983.K497   1990
822.3'3—dc20   89-77518
                                         CIP

Printed in the United States of America

To my family

HOLY SPIRIT LIBRARY
92 0280

CONTENTS

PREFACE

JOHN DRYDEN praised Shakespeare for his "universal mind, that comprehended all characters and passions." The faithfulness to actual experience of the characters and passions Shakespeare represents and their ability to illuminate our own lives are among the main reasons we continue to be moved by his plays and to value them so highly. Much of the recent criticism of Shakespeare, about which I shall have more to say in the concluding chapter, "Shakespeare's Humanism," either denies or ignores this kind of enduring mimetic truth in Shakespeare, finding more meaning in Elizabethan cultural contingencies than in the plays themselves. The purpose of this book, which evolved as a series of articles on the major tragedies, is to renew an appreciation of the timelessness of Shakespeare's genius in dramatizing human actions and feelings. Drawing upon medieval and Renaissance religious ideas as well as both Renaissance and modern conceptions of character, it explores Shakespeare's dramatization of the emotional and spiritual suffering of the heroes in *Hamlet*, *Othello*, *Macbeth*, and *King Lear*.

The articles from which chapters 2–6 are drawn are: "Hamlet's Grief," *ELH* 48 (1981); "The Polarization of Erotic Love in *Othello*," *Modern Language Review* 73 (1978), reprinted in *Shakespeare and the Experience of Love* (Cambridge: Cambridge Univ. Press, 1981); "Macbeth's Suicide," *ELH* 51 (1984); and "The

Emotional Landscape of *King Lear,*" *Shakespeare Quarterly* 39 (1988). I wish to thank the editors of *ELH, Modern Language Review,* and *Shakespeare Quarterly* for their kind permission to reprint the material that originally appeared in these journals. Portions of all four chapters were also published in abbreviated form in an encyclopedia essay on "Shakespeare's Tragedies," in *William Shakespeare: His World, His Work, His Influence,* ed. John Andrews (New York: Charles Scribner's Sons: 1985). I have revised all of these pieces to emphasize their common assumptions and cumulative argument. Chapters 1 and 6 elaborate this larger argument and place it in the context of the present state of Shakespeare criticism.

The University of Virginia generously gave me time to write. I am indebted to generations of both undergraduate and graduate students in my Shakespeare seminars and to many colleagues and friends. The late Irvin Ehrenpreis, Lester Beaurline, Paul Cantor, Alastair Fowler, E. D. Hirsch, James Nohrnberg, Robert Kellogg, and Stephen Orgel read parts of the book and gave me valuable criticism, and I am grateful to Martin Battestin for his encouragement. Jeffrey Cox, Joyce Van Dyke, and James Rubin helped me crystallize some of my ideas at an early stage. I owe most to my wife Beverly.

THE PASSIONS OF SHAKESPEARE'S

TRAGIC HEROES

CHAPTER 1

"FOR HE WAS

GREAT OF HEART"

I N HIS ACCOUNT OF A PERFORMANCE of *Macbeth* at the Globe in
1611, the Elizabethan astrologer and playgoer Simon Forman
focused on the action, its high moments as well as its subtle cau-
sations. But what he seems to have remembered most vividly (he
gives it his longest description) is Macbeth's reaction to Banquo's
ghost in the banquet scene. In treating this moment in the play,
he comments not only upon the event and its place in the evolv-
ing action, but upon Macbeth's state of mind. He writes that
when Macbeth "sawe the goste of banco, which fronted him so,"
he "fell into a great passion of fear and fury." [1] The phrase speaks
clearly enough across the centuries—as indicative a stage direc-
tion for the actor now as it would have been then—and it
discriminates the emotional keynote of Macbeth's whole characterization: not just its particularity, its peculiar conjunction of
hesitancy and rashness, dread and anger, but equally important
its magnitude, what Forman calls its greatness.

Forman's term at the same time has specifically Elizabethan
connotations. For the majority of Renaissance moral philosophers, as for earlier Christian and classical writers, the passions,
"the passions of the mind" as they were called, comprehended
the whole spectrum of human emotions, including the realm
of the imagination. The concupiscible "power" of the soul, which
moves it to "follow that which the *Soule* thinketh to be good for

it, or to flie that which it takes to be evill," was considered to spawn three pairs of contrary passions—love and hatred, desire and aversion, joy and sadness.[2] The irascible power of the soul, which tries to overcome impediments to the operation of the concupiscible power was also considered to generate three groups of passions—hope and despair, fear and daring, and anger, whose contrary was not a passion of the "sensitive" part of the soul, but belonged rather to what Prospero, when he resolves in *The Tempest* to forgive his enemies, calls the "nobler reason" (5.1.26).[3]

In this ancient schema, the passions did not usually emerge as subjects of approval. Human passions, and especially the kind of inordinate passion Forman seems to note with wonder in Macbeth, were considered perturbations in the Renaissance, ultimately expressions of "the infected root of originall sinne," the imperfection in man's nature that both caused the Fall and constituted his state forever after it.[4] Pierre de La Primaudaye's *The French Academie*, an extensive and well-known treatise of moral psychology first translated into English in 1586, offers a typical homiletic elucidation of these assumptions:

> THE PHILOSOPHERS teach us by their writings; and experience doth better shew it unto us, that to covet and desire is proper to the soule, and that from thence all the affections and desires of men proceede, which draw them hither and thither diversly, that they may attaine to that thing, which they thinke is able to leade them to the enjoying of some good, whereby they may live a contented and happie life. Which felicitie, the most part of men, through a false opinion, or ignorance rather of that which is good, and by following the inclination of their corrupted nature, do seeke and labor to find in humane and earthlie things, as in riches, glorie, honor, and pleasure. But forasmuch as the enjoying of these things doth not bring with it sufficient cause of contentation, they perceive themselves alwaies deprived of the end of their desires, and are constrained to wander all their life time beyond all bounds and measure, according to the

rashnes and inconstancie of their lusts. And although they rejoice for a little while at everie new change, yet presently they loath the selfesame thing, which not long before they earnestly desired. Their owne estate alwaies seemeth unto them to be woorst, and everie present condition of life, to be burdensome. From one estate they seeke after another.[5]

La Primaudaye's assumptions are traditionally Christian and moralistic, and his ensuing accounts of the various passions, like those of many of his contemporaries, are often conventional. But if the observations are not originally his, they are not therefore uninteresting or unobservant. Most of what he and his contemporaries have to say about human nature and behavior is true, and their anatomies, if not always valuations, of human emotions inform the unsurpassed psychological sophistication of a writer like Montaigne, upon whom some of the later French moral commentators themselves drew.[6] They also inform the representation of human feeling and behavior in Shakespearian drama.

The biblical sense of the mutability and vanity, as well as force, of human passion, of which La Primaudaye speaks, for example, is endemic and deep in Shakespeare's plays. In the comedies, from the earlier romantic comedies, through the problem plays to the final romances, the attitude toward passion is cautionary, and the goal of the action tends to be the achievement of temperance. In *The Merchant of Venice*, for example, Portia actually schools her passion for Bassanio as he prepares to choose the lead casket:

How all the other passions fleet to air,
As doubtful thoughts, and rash-embraced despair,
And shudd'ring fear, and green-eyed jealousy.
O love, be moderate! Allay thy ecstasy.
In measure rain thy joy; scant this excess.
I feel too much thy blessing: make it less,
For fear I surfeit.   (3.2.108–14)

Claudio expresses a similar attitude, in a harsher key, in an astringent speech in *Measure for Measure:*

> As surfeit is the father of much fast,
> So every scope, by the immoderate use,
> Turns to restraint. Our natures do pursue,
> Like rats that raven down their proper bane,
> A thirsty evil; and when we drink, we die.   (1.2.118–22)

He is referring to sexual passion, the play's particular preoccupation, but the lines have a resonance that subsumes the entire tragicomic texture of the problem comedy. The same motif of temperance informs the emotional, if not spiritual, movement of the last plays, where potentially tragic passions, though often enacted, are comically depleted or tempered. The murderous lust that lies behind Posthumus's jealousy in *Cymbeline,* for example, is purged by being acted out and displaced onto his farcically grotesque double, Cloten.[7] In *The Tempest* a portion of Prospero's anger is acted out in the imaginary ordeals of the court party and the physical punishment of Stephano, Trinculo, and Caliban, but not the whole of it, and the sea change that he and other characters "suffer" (1.2.404) is more difficult and complex. Prospero says to Ariel, who has been moved by the distress of Prospero's kinsmen:

> Hast thou, which art but air, a touch, a feeling
> Of their afflictions, and shall not myself,
> One of their kind, that relish all as sharply
> Passion as they, be kindlier mov'd than thou art?
> Though with their high wrongs I am struck to th' quick,
> Yet with my nobler reason 'gainst my fury
> Do I take part. The rarer action is
> In virtue than in vengeance.   (5.1.21–28)

A large measure of the Renaissance psychology of the passions lies behind Prospero's resolution of his anger and desire for revenge, and as the source of these lines in Montaigne's essay "Of

Cruelty" unequivocally confirms,[8] his action is rare not because he transcends his fury and forgives his enemies out of goodness, which is an attribute of God, but because his human virtue enables him to work through and temper his passion. The incipient passion that marks Prospero's characterization for most of the play—his continuously "beating mind," his irascibility not only with Caliban but with Ferdinand and Ariel and even Miranda—authenticates this achievement of temperance and forgiveness rather than questions or devalues it.

Similar attitudes toward temperance and the passions are expressed in the tragedies. When Romeo, as he anticipates his marriage with Juliet, tells the Friar:

> But come what sorrow can,
> It cannot countervail the exchange of joy
> That one short minute gives me in her sight.
> Do thou but close our hands with holy words,
> Then love-devouring death do what he dare—
> It is enough I may but call her mine;

the Friar answers:

> These violent delights have violent ends,
> And in their triumph die like fire and powder,
> Which as they kiss consume. The sweetest honey
> Is loathsome in his own deliciousness,
> And in the taste confounds the appetite.
> Therefore love moderately. Long love doth so.
> Too swift arrives as tardy as too slow. (2.5.3–15)

At the center of Hamlet, in language that resembles the Friar's, the Player King says:

> What to ourselves in passion we propose,
> The passion ending, doth the purpose lose.
> The violence of either grief or joy
> Their own enactures with themselves destroy. (3.2.185–88)

Hamlet himself explicitly endorses these ideas. He tells Horatio that he has chosen him as a friend, because

> thou hast been
> As one in suff'ring all that suffers nothing,
> A man that Fortune's buffets and rewards
> Hath ta'en with equal thanks; and blest are those
> Whose blood and judgment are so well commingled
> That they are not a pipe for Fortune's finger
> To sound what stop she please. Give me that man
> That is not passion's slave, and I will wear him
> In my heart's core, ay, in my heart of heart,
> As I do thee.   (3.2.63–72)

These sentiments, however, have a much different perspective in Shakespeare's tragedies than they do in his comedies and romances. The Friar may be correct, and Horatio may be a Renaissance model as well as Hamlet's, but neither can be mistaken for a tragic hero. In the "intensification of the life they share with others," as A. C. Bradley observed, it is precisely intemperance, the "marked one-sidedness," the identification of "the whole being" with one passion, that most characterizes the heroes in Shakespeare's tragedies.[9] The blaze of erotic passion, initially perhaps partly funny but eventually almost intrusively grave, is what defines Romeo and Juliet as moving tragic figures, and the vulnerability to passion and suffering is what distinguishes Hamlet as a tragic hero and compels our own deepest imaginative sympathies. As A. P. Rossiter remarked in an excellent and neglected essay, "Shakespeare's conception of tragedy plainly and constantly concerns the man who *is* 'passion's slave.'"[10] All the heroes of Shakespeare's tragedies—and especially those of the four titanic plays *Hamlet, Othello, Macbeth,* and *King Lear*—suffer to the heart's core and suffer everything in suffering all. "Suffering," as Rossiter says, "beyond solace, beyond any moral palliation, and suffering because of a human greatness which is great because great in passion: that, above everything else, is central to Shakespeare's tragic conception."[11]

The heart was generally considered to be the seat of the passions in the Renaissance, and the passionate movement of the heart is at the center of all four of the great tragedies. Hamlet, for example, is probably most often admired for his intellectual energy, for the copiousness and eloquence of his thoughts. But we have to remember, as Hamlet is always compelled to remember, that behind these thoughts, and usually their occasion, is a continuous and tremendous experience of pain and suffering. As he himself tells us, it is his heart that he unpacks with words; it is against what he calls the "heartache" (3.1.64) of human existence that he protests in his most famous soliloquy (and this is the first use of the term in that sense the *OED* records); and it is the heart's core, the heart of heart, of which he is always conscious. Hamlet's "noble heart" is what the temperate Horatio first pays tribute to at the moment of his death (5.2.312), and in an almost literal sense the "heart of [his] mystery" (3.2.353–54) is what we ourselves are most interested in.

Othello also, and obviously, is permeated by the language of the heart. Brabantio dies of his "bruised heart" (1.3.218); Emilia says her heart is "full" (5.2.182) just before her own death, when she turns against Iago; and Iago himself, interestingly, talks repeatedly of the heart he hides. Desdemona is presented from first to last in the play as a woman of steadfast and loving heart: "My heart's subdued / Even to the very quality of my lord" (1.3.250–51). Othello himself, finally, is always defined by his heart, in his rage and eventual despair, as well as in his love. He draws from Desdemona the "prayer of earnest heart" to tell the story that initiates their courtship (1.3.151); at the apogee of their reunion on the shores of Cyprus, he says, "And this, (*they kiss*), and this, the greatest discords be / That e'er our hearts shall make" (2.1.199–200); and it is because he has so completely, as he says, "garnered up my heart" (4.2.59) in Desdemona that his collapse is intelligible as well as appalling. He says during that collapse that his "heart is turned to stone" (4.1.178–79), but though that may be his wish it is never his achievement, which is what gives stature to him even in his savagery. When he commits suicide, Cassio's epitaph is proper: "This did I fear, but thought he had no weapon, / For he was great of heart" (5.2.370–71).

Macbeth, as we have seen, is especially remembered by Forman for his "great passion," and passions of the heart (and their cauterization) mark the whole course of his tragic career, as well as of Lady Macbeth's. At first apparently immune to feelings, by the time of the sleepwalking scene Lady Macbeth's heart has become "sorely charged" by them: "I would not have such a heart in my bosom," her attendant says, "for the dignity of the whole body" (5.1.51–53). Macbeth's tragedy begins when his "seated heart knock[s] at [his] ribs" (1.3.135). The famous literal knocking at the gates after the murder of Duncan is in part a reverberation of that state of emotion, and Macbeth's tragic career is punctuated by references to the heart. When he resolves to murder Macduff's family, he says, "The very firstlings of my heart shall be / The firstlings of my hand" (4.1.163–64), a statement, as we shall see, that has particular and extraordinary force in the play, and at the end he tells Seyton, what is once again literalized in the state of Scotland, that he is "sick at heart" (5.3.21). Scotland's recovery from that sickness is significantly heralded by Macduff's feeling for the loss of his family, a feeling that Malcolm successfully, if also callowly, urges Macduff to convert to rage: "Let grief / Convert to anger: blunt not the heart, enrage it" (4.3.230–31).

Finally, the word *heart* itself resonates in *King Lear*, describing the extremes of the play's characterizations, from the "honest-hearted" Kent (1.4.19) to the "marble-hearted" ingratitude and "hard-hearts" of Goneril and Regan (1.4.237; 3.6.36).[12] "Heart" is the metonym for Lear himself in the storm—"poor old heart, he holp the heavens to rain" (3.7.60)—and it is the primary register of Lear's experience. He rejects Cordelia because she cannot heave her "heart" into her "mouth" (1.1.92) and he pronounces her banishment as the divorce of her heart from his own: "So be my grave my peace as here I give / Her father's heart from her" (1.1.125–26), an uncanny line that predicates his eventual reunion with her in death. The heart is physically palpable to Lear. He says he is "struck . . . upon the very heart" by Goneril's "tongue" (2.2.333–34), and the same tactile sense of the heart emerges in the synapse between physical and emotional pain that prompts the first movement of fellow feeling in him:

My wits begin to turn.
(*To Fool*) Come on, my boy. How dost, my boy? Art cold?
I am cold myself. . . .
Poor fool and knave, I have one part in my heart
That's sorry yet for thee.   (3.2.67–69, 72–73)

As Lear moves toward madness, he recognizes that his rage against Cordelia drew from his "heart all love" and "wrenched" his "frame of nature / From the fixed place" (1.4.247–48); he then repeatedly identifies his incipient madness with his heart: "O, how this mother swells up toward my heart! / *Histerica passio* down, thou climbing sorrow" (2.2.231–32); "O me, my heart! My rising heart! But down" (2.2.292); "But this heart shall break into a hundred thousand flaws / Or ere I'll weep" (2.2.458–59). The breaking of the heart "into a hundred thousand flaws" defines the point toward which most references to the heart in *Lear* eventually move, and as we shall see, it suggests the extremity of pain and suffering that is the play's peculiar concern, most particularly in its depiction of Lear's relation to the faithful and loving daughter whose very name is the heart.

Richard Burbage, the premier actor of Shakespeare's company, was praised in a contemporary elegy for his capacity to become the characters he played, and the elegist singled out his sympathetic portrayals of "kind Leer," the "greved Moor," and the "sadd lover" Hamlet.[13] These descriptions, like many others in theatrical criticism of the time, suggest the essential propriety of sympathizing, if not identifying, with the passions and suffering of Shakespeare's heroes. As A. C. Bradley wrote, "We might not object to the statement that Lear deserved to suffer for his folly, selfishness and tyranny, but to assert that he deserved to suffer what he did suffer is to do violence to any healthy moral sense." "Our everyday legal and moral notions" "of justice and desert" are "in *all* cases, even those of Richard III and of Macbeth and Lady Macbeth, untrue to our imaginative experience. When we are immersed in a tragedy, we feel towards dispositions, actions, and persons such emotions as attraction and repulsion, pity, wonder, fear, horror, perhaps hatred; but we do not *judge*." "We watch what is," Bradley continued, "seeing that so it happened,

and must have happened, feeling that it is piteous, dreadful, aw-
ful, mysterious, but neither passing sentence on the agents, nor
asking whether the behaviour of the ultimate power towards
them is just. And, therefore, the use of such language in attempts
to render our imaginative experience in terms of the understanding is, to say the least, full of danger." [14]

Since Renaissance moral (as opposed to theatrical) commentators on the passions do habitually use such language and do
habitually judge, Bradley's remarks suggest the need to separate
their analyses of passion and suffering from their homiletic judgments of them. Lily B. Campbell's important early study, *Shakespeare's Tragic Heroes: Slaves of Passion* suffers from the failure to
make this distinction. [15] In his comedies as well as his tragedies
Shakespeare's representation of human experience is always mul-
tivalent. The same Friar who chastises the excess of Romeo's passion for Juliet remarks that

> The earth, that's nature's mother, is her tomb.
> What is her burying grave, that is her womb,
> And from her womb children of divers kind
> We sucking on her natural bosom find,
> Many for many virtues excellent,
> None but for some, and yet all different.
> O mickle is the powerful grace that lies
> In plants, herbs, stones, and their true qualities,
> For naught so vile that on the earth doth live
> But to the earth some special good doth give;
> Nor aught so good but, strained from that fair use,
> Revolts from true birth, stumbling on abuse.
> Virtue itself turns vice being misapplied,
> And vice sometime's by action dignified.   (2.2.9–22)

Perhaps no other Renaissance writer, with the exception of Montaigne, expresses so catholic an understanding of human behavior, and in approaching his tragedies it is better to err on the side
of Bradley's biases than those of the Renaissance moralists.

It is best of all, however, to try to achieve a balance. As William Empson pointed out, the distinction of Elizabethan drama,

and Shakespeare's preeminently, is its combination of sympathy and judgment, engagement and detachment.[16] The differing emotions that Bradley says we feel toward the hero are a result of a constant interplay of empathy and judgment in our responses to him, and the disengaging paradoxes of the Friar's statement rest, of course, upon a foundation of normative moral expectations. Though passions can indeed be said to "spin the plot" of Shakespearean tragedy, as the Victorians thought, Shakespeare does not sentimentalize the passions, still less glamorize them. There is a pervasive counterpoint of irony in all of Shakespeare's representations of his tragic heroes, which the morally clinical Renaissance anatomies of the passions simply make explicit. This irony is in a large sense "comic," but it only exacerbates the passions of the heroes. For Shakespeare's heroes not only are obviously subject to the evanescence of human passion, but they also consciously protest against it, and that consciousness and ultimately unavailing protest constitute a substantial part of their suffering. One can reasonably imagine that Hamlet himself, for example, may have written the Player King's lines, but in any case their truth is a continuous torment to him (as well as, interestingly, to the Ghost, who is clearly more disturbed by the inconstancy of Gertrude than by the usurpation of his crown). Hamlet's exclamation "frailty, thy name is woman" (1.2.146) is a specific indictment of his mother's hasty remarriage, but it is at the same time an outcry against the mutability and decay of human affection of which her action is only an example, a condition of life that he cannot bring himself to accept until very near the end of the play and of his own life. And the experience of such decay, as we shall see, informs his relations to Ophelia and Rosencrantz and Guildenstern as well.

Othello too protests against the limits and impermanence of affections, and his protest is no less powerful because it is based on a partially self-created delusion. It is in fact more powerful and more painful because Desdemona's love, like that of the heroines in the romances, offers the promise of the transcendence of the mutability of passion that tragedy usually does not provide or provides only in death. The sources of Othello's decomposition are manifold, but not the least important is the boundlessness of his love. His claim that he loved Desdemona "too well" (5.2.353) may be partly self-justification, but it is also true, and it accounts for why the thought of her mutability becomes so destructive. There are, no doubt, other and more sensible ways of dealing with a wife whom one thinks is unfaithful, but Othello's, though horrifying, is proper to his tragedy and a function of his heroism. Othello says of Desdemona,

> Perdition catch my soul
> But I do love thee! And when I love thee not,
> Chaos is come again. (3.3.92–94)

Such chaos does come in no small measure because of the vicissitudes of Othello's own emotional life, but it comes also, as we shall see, because such vicissitudes, a condition of adult existence, are those which, in his idealism and absoluteness, he tries to transcend.

The same is true of Macbeth, though with a different inflection. Both he and Lady Macbeth directly endure the emptiness of passion, "where," as Lady Macbeth remarks, "our desire is got without content" (3.2.7), and that motif, a favorite of the homilists, is enacted over and over again in *Macbeth*, including in the Porter's speech about drink, which "provokes the desire but ... takes away the performance" (2.3.28–29). But the experience of the insatiability of desire is exponentially acute in Macbeth, as we shall see, because it is the very gap between the consciousness of desire and its achievement, again a condition of human existence, against which Macbeth sets himself and which makes him actually wish for death. "Better be with the dead," he says soon after killing Duncan and becoming king,

> Whom we to gain our peace have sent to peace,
> Than on the torture of the mind to lie
> In restless ecstasy. (3.2.21–24)

The lines are an epigraph to his whole tragic career.

The suffering caused by the consciousness of the mutability

of passion, finally, is everywhere evident in *Lear.* It virtually defines all those who are good in the play, and it is the substance of the experience of Lear and Gloucester, both of whom suffer the betrayal of their children but are most tormented by the consciousness of the mutability and limits of their own affections. Gloucester is literally blinded by the appetite that created Edmond, but his heart is said to burst at his death, "twixt two extremes of passion, joy and grief" (5.3.190) in his reunion with Edgar, the son whom he loves and whom he denied. Lear, similarly is enraged by the ingratitude of Goneril and Regan, by the question that echoes through the play: "Is there any cause in nature that makes these hard-hearts?" (3.6.35–36); but he is actually driven mad, as the Fool makes searingly clear, by his consciousness of his denial of his own love for Cordelia, and his reunion with her in death is coordinate with the breaking of his heart as well.

Lear's agony especially crystallizes the peculiarly tragic power of the representation of the passions in all the tragedies, because behind the suffering consciousness of all Shakespeare's tragic heroes is a protest against the reality of which the frailty and decay of human passion is itself an image, the reality of human mortality. As Northrop Frye has said, "The basis of the tragic vision is being in time" in which "death is, not an incident in life, not even the inevitable end of life, but the essential event that gives shape and form to life." This ironic apprehension, he argues, is complemented by "a counter-movement of being that we call heroic, a capacity for action or passion, for doing or suffering, which is above ordinary human experience." He concludes that "in tragedy the ironic vision survives the heroic one, but the heroic vision is the one we remember, and the tragedy is for its sake."[17]

Frye's conception has a particular cogency in understanding the representation of suffering and of the passions in Shakespeare. The passions of the mind were often explicitly associated with man's mortality in Elizabethan thinking, and in Shakespeare the display of passion, which is often simultaneously heroic and ironic, is always ultimately informed by the apprehension of the immanence of death. It is explicit in Romeo's dialogue with the

Friar, in his presentiment of "love-devouring death," and in the answering puns on dying and sexual consummation that emerge in the Friar's homily. That these commonplace Elizabethan puns on "die" are literalized in the action of the play hardly needs demonstration. The Prologue invites us to watch "the fearful passage of" Romeo and Juliet's "death-marked love," and there is a clear intimation that the love is "death-marked" in the sense not only that it is foredoomed, but also that death may be its cognate state, if not its goal. This perspective is supported by the lovers' repeated premonitions of disaster, by the many references associating the marriage bed with the grave, and of course by the enactment of the final scene, the last of the love scenes, in the tomb, the "triumphant grave," the "feasting presence," Romeo says, made "full of light" by Juliet's beauty (5.3.83, 86). Both Romeo and Juliet commingle images of their passion and death, Romeo suggesting that death itself has become Juliet's lover and Juliet treating the dagger with which she stabs herself as an erotic object. Both lovers die with a kiss.

Othello, which to some extent internalizes the external circumstances of *Romeo and Juliet* into the soul of the hero, also mingles images of love and death. Othello says to Desdemona, when he is first reunited with her in Cyprus,

> If it were now to die
> 'Twere now to be most happy, for I fear
> My soul hath her content so absolute
> That not another comfort like to this
> Succeeds in unknown fate.   (2.1.190–94)

The speech is highly reminiscent of Romeo's lines to the Friar linking the "exchange of joy" with death, and at this point in the play it is less a reflection of Othello's own psychology, one of his alleged insufficiencies, than it is a reflection, in his characterization, of the mortal undertow of passion that is common to all the tragedies. As in *Romeo and Juliet*, but even more literally, the marriage bed in *Othello* becomes the bride's funeral bier; and like the lovers in the earlier play, Othello himself dies "upon a kiss" (5.2.369). Othello's love, like Romeo's (though far more complexly), is always "death-marked," as he himself suggests when he stands over her body at the end of the play: "Here is my journey's end, here is my butt, / And very sea-mark of my utmost sail" (5.2.274–75).

The inherent association of passion and death in *Macbeth*, though perhaps less obvious, is equally significant. It is possible to forget in reading, though hardly in performance, that the play is awash in blood, and of course Macbeth's "great passion of fear and fury" is itself continuously murderous. But there is another and more important sense in which passion and death are associated in the play, for as I have already suggested and shall later argue in detail, it is the very uncertainty and insatiability of passion in human life that Macbeth cannot tolerate and against which he tries to act. This is what gives such intricacy to his characterization. The usual critical question about *Macbeth* is how we can sympathize with a hero who is so barbaric. The more interesting question, it seems to me, is how Shakespeare can maintain our sympathy for a hero who is deliberating draining himself of emotion. Part of the answer, which Renaissance conceptions of passion can help make intelligible, is that in Macbeth we watch a man whose conscious wish is to accelerate the natural self-consumption of passion, to find "peace" with the dead. We watch a suicide.

In *Hamlet* and *King Lear*, finally, death is itself the manifest and most important subject of passion. With an egotism—the Renaissance would have called it presumption—that marks all the tragic heroes, Hamlet says: "The time is out of joint. O cursed spite, / That ever I was born to set it right!" (1.5.189–90). This is the injunction of the Ghost and of the revenge play genre itself, but insofar as it is a reflection of Hamlet's character, it is also a protest against death, and not only that of his father. As I have already suggested, it is the mortality of which his mother's remarriage is an instance as well as a result that most animates him, as from the first, it is his own mortality and limits that he must come to accept, as he does finally and perspicuously in the last act when he accepts the "special providence in the fall of a sparrow" (5.2.165–66). Hamlet's passion, as we shall see, is grief, its anger as well as its sorrow.

King Lear, a play that is primarily concerned with two very old and dying men, is even more deeply, if sometimes less obviously, informed by a protest against death. Lear's rage, his prevailing passion, is ostensibly against the mutability of affection that he sees in his daughters and in himself, but at root, as I shall try to show, it is a passionate denial of what his abdication nominally acknowledges, his own impending death. Edgar tells Gloucester,

> Men must endure
> Their going hence even as their coming hither.
> Ripeness is all.
>
> (5.2.9–11)

Both Gloucester and Lear do in fact exhaustively "endure" the truth of this homily, as Edgar himself realizes, when he says in the closing lines that we should

> Speak what we feel, not what we ought to say.
> The oldest hath borne most. We that are young
> Shall never see so much, nor live so long. (5.3.300–302)

In Ecclesiastes, upon which I think Shakespeare drew deeply in *King Lear*, the Preacher, whose focus is also upon the transitoriness of human bonds and the immanence of death in human life, remarks that "he that encreaseth knowledge encreaseth sorrow" (1:18).[18] It is this peculiarly passionate "knowledge" that is the substance of Shakespearian tragedy and the subject of this book.

In the chapters that follow, I draw upon Freud, as well as Renaissance and earlier Christian texts, in interpreting the passions and suffering of Hamlet, Othello, Macbeth, and Lear. Justifications of the use of such ideas do not usually disarm critics who are hostile to them (they often only provide ammunition), and the interpretations must finally speak for themselves. But I do not wish to write only for initiates of Freudian or Christian criticism—I am not myself committed to either as an ideology—and some preliminary explanation of my critical approach may be helpful. To begin with, Shakespeare's heroes are often regressively childlike, which is what can make their passions at once awesome and ironic, if not grotesque, and Freud's explorations of the origins of adult behavior in early childhood are peculiarly suited to help explain the dramatic power as well as psychological integrity of this combination. Moreover, Freud's range is far greater than is usually recognized. In addition to the subject of sexuality, with which he tends to be too reductively identified, he writes with enduring insights about human growth, about many adult as well as childish emotions and ways of thinking, about the feeling of being in love, about grief, about the way human beings try to deny their mortality, about the very processes of human passions and suffering. The Bible too reflects upon such experiences, and Shakespeare of course represents them. To the extent that he and the Bible and Freud are true to these experiences, they have insights in common that can be explored, legitimately and interestingly. Moreover, as I shall suggest in a moment, the allegorical detritus of Shakespearian (and biblical) representations of character makes them more, rather than less, susceptible to a modern understanding of depth psychology.

I also assume that however considerable the cultural differences between Shakespeare's age and ours may be, there are also, and have to be, significant similarities in order for us to understand anything about earlier times and texts. In his admirable book *A New Mimesis*, A. D. Nuttall remarks that Shakespeare himself anticipates the results of many "seemingly modern tools of thought, such as the concepts of cultural history," and that "the easiest way—no, the *only* way—to account for this is to say that Shakespeare was looking very hard at the same world (400 years younger, but still the same world) that we are looking at now." [19] It seems to me, in addition, that culture, in any case, does not entirely determine the fundamental passions of an individual human life; that individuals in the Renaissance had particular as well as representative emotional lives that we can understand; and finally, that the revelation of such emotional life is at the heart of Shakespeare's great tragedies and of their continuing power to move us. These propositions all go against the grain of much recent modern criticism, and I shall return to them in the concluding chapter of this book. I hope, however, that they will be most validated for the reader as I practice them, in my interpretations of the plays.

At the same time, I want to make clear that I sympathize with such contentions as Nuttall's that the use of what he calls Freud's "images" in literary criticism is often more "ornamental" than "corroborative," since these images "seem seldom to function in a genuinely heuristic manner." I think there is also some truth to his assertion that in the depiction of human behavior "Freud is the allegorist, Shakespeare the psychologist."[20] It is certainly evident that psychoanalytic (as well as theological) interpretations of Shakespeare are often, if not habitually, reductive, doctrinaire, and remote both in tone and substance from the kind of experience Shakespeare gives us. But unlike Nuttall, I think these problems can be modulated as long as a critic does not displace an interest in Shakespeare's text with an interest in Freudian or Christian thought (which seems to me to be the most endemic failing of both theological and psychoanalytic critics) and as long as he or she looks on the text, as Jean Starobinski suggests, with a "gaze of knowledge that is also the gaze of love," rather than the gaze of Actaeon upon Diana, the gaze of "sacrilegious indiscretion" and of "aggression."[21] Freudian and Christian ideas do not have to be applied clinically, in a diagnostic, if not predatory, hunt for pathology. They can instead be used to enhance our understanding of the experiences which the plays both represent and elicit from us. The Bible is not simply a long homily, and Freud was from the first interested in explaining normal human behavior as well as emotional illness. Freudian and Christian ideas are far more humane and illuminating than the uses to which literary critics have usually put them, and they can help explain why his plays continue to be so alive and to reach so wide an audience of spectators and readers.

There is historical warrant for such an approach. Christian images, of course, pervaded Shakespeare's culture, and throughout his career he obviously thought in terms of them. If those images are themselves frequently allegorical, then we should consider the extent to which the allegories are incorporated into the living texture of Shakespeare's creations. The medieval drama that was his inheritance provided a model for just such a creative transmutation of Christian allegory into theatrical life. The morality play especially, though by definition a homiletic presentation of the moral struggle between personified virtues and vices for the soul of man, is also at the same time an intrapsychic drama, a depiction in concrete images of an action *within* the soul of the play's protagonist. The moralities present a mental landscape that is, at least incipiently, as psychological as it is moral. As I have suggested elsewhere,[22] the unique staging of such a play as *The Castle of Perseverance*, for example, is itself interesting. The image presented in the drawing that has come down to us—of Mankind's castle, with his bed under it, surrounded by the scaffolds of God, the World, the Flesh, Belial, and Covetousness—literalizes the scaffolding of a human life and reflects the same allegorical impulse, if not essentially the same mental topography, that is to be found in Freud's diagrams depicting the composition of the human psyche. In any event, the action of the play evokes such a topography with great scope as well as richness of concrete detail. We witness the panorama of Mankind's spiritual progress from birth to death and judgment, and in the course of that progress we are introduced to virtually all, to borrow Dr. Johnson's praise of Shakespeare, "those general passions and principles by which all minds are agitated, and the whole system of life is continued in motion."[23] The cast of characters alone presents us with a conspectus of elemental human experience: Belial, and with him Pride, Wrath, and Envy; Flesh, and with him Gluttony, Lechery, and Sloth, Covetousness, Backbiter; Shrift, Penitence; Meekness, Patience, Charity, Temperance, Chastity, Business, and Generosity; Death, the Soul (after Mankind's death); Mercy, Truth, Righteousness, and Peace; the Father sitting on his throne.

Mankind himself, Humanum Genus, and with him the Good Angel and the Bad Angel, does not interact with all the characters, but he is nonetheless ultimately inseparable from almost everything that happens in the play. Most of the action is not only about him, it constitutes him. He exists as a separate character, with all the definition and vitality an actor could give him, but he is also, if not finally, made up of the primitive impulses and energies of the forces that are represented in the characters surrounding him. The play as a whole thus composes as well as decomposes his "personality." The characters, the set, and the action are visualizations of the processes of his experience.

Such allegorizations of human experience accustomed medieval audiences to a way of understanding the primitive components and dynamics of human behavior, that Freud, in a sense, had to recover through psychoanalytic excavation. This understanding is shown to a significant degree in Renaissance moral psychologies of the passions, and persists as well, without necessarily entailing moral judgments, in Elizabethan drama, both in the psychomachic structure of the characterization of the hero and in the remnants of popular parts of the psychomachia, especially the Vice. The joining of Freudian and Renaissance ideas in interpreting Shakespeare's portrayal of the emotional and spiritual life of his tragic heroes, therefore, makes historical as well as critical sense.

CHAPTER II

HAMLET

H AMLET IS A REVENGE PLAY, and judging by the number of performances, parodies, and editions of *The Spanish Tragedy* alone, the genre enjoyed an extraordinary popularity on the Elizabethan stage. Part of the reason for that popularity is the theatrical power of the revenge motif itself. The quest for vengeance satisfies an audience's most primitive wishes for intrigue and violence. "The Tragic Auditory," as Charles Lamb once remarked, "wants blood,"[1] and the revenge motif satisfies it in abundance. Equally important, it gives significant shape to the plot and sustained energy to the action, whatever moral calculus one may use in judging the ethos of revenge itself.[2] But if vengeance composes the plot of the revenge play, grief composes its essential emotional content, its substance. In Marlowe's *Jew of Malta*, when Ferneze finds the body of his son killed in a duel, he cries out in his loss that he wishes his son had been murdered so that he could avenge his death.[3] It is a casual line, but it suggests a deep connection between anger and sorrow in the revenge-play genre itself that both Kyd and Shakespeare draw upon profoundly. At the end of *The Spanish Tragedy* the ghost of Andrea says, "Ay, now my hopes have end in their effects, / When blood and sorrow finish my desires" (4.5.1–2),[4] and it was unquestionably Kyd's brilliance in representing the elemental power of sorrow, as well as of blood, that enabled the revenge genre to establish so large a claim on the Elizabethan theatrical imagination. The speeches in which Hieronimo gives voice to his grief, including the famous "Oh eyes, no eyes, but fountains fraught with tears; / Oh life, no life, but lively form of death" (3.2.1–2) were parodied for decades after their first performance, so great was their impact, and the moving figure of an old man maddened with grief over the loss of his son was a major part of Shakespeare's theatrical inheritance.

In Shakespeare's play it is Hamlet himself who talks explicitly of sorrow and blood, relating them directly to the ghost as well as to each other in the scene in his mother's bedchamber in which the ghost appears for the last time. "Look you," he tells his mother, who characteristically cannot see the ghost,

> how pale he glares.
> His form and cause conjoined, preaching to stones,
> Would make them capable. (*To the Ghost*) Do not look upon
> me,
> Lest with this piteous action you convert
> My stern effects. Then what I have to do
> Will want true colour—tears perchance for blood.
>
> (3.4.116–21)

These lines suggest synapses between grief and vengeance that can help make the whole relation between the plot and emotional content of *Hamlet* more intelligible, and that particularly can help answer the charge made by many distinguished critics that Hamlet's emotions seem in excess of any objective cause as well as of the plot. T. S. Eliot's remark, for example, that Hamlet's mother is not an adequate equivalent for his disgust with her, that no possible action can satisfy this disgust, and that therefore "nothing that Shakespeare can do with the plot can express Hamlet for him" are at least susceptible to an answer if we take seriously Hamlet's own focus upon the experience of grief and upon its profound interaction with his task of revenge.[5]

The note of grief is sounded by Hamlet in his first words in the play, before he ever sees the ghost, in his opening dialogue with the King and his mother. The Queen says to him:

Good Hamlet, cast thy nightly colour off,
And let thine eye look like a friend on Denmark.
Do not for ever with thy vailèd lids
Seek for thy noble father in the dust.
Thou know'st 'tis common—all that lives must die,
Passing through nature to eternity.   (1.2.68–73)

Hamlet answers, "Ay, madam, it is common." "If it be / Why
seems it so particular with thee?" she asks; and he responds,

Seems, madam? Nay, it *is*. I know not "seems."
'Tis not alone my inky cloak, good-mother.
Nor customary suits of solemn black,
Nor windy suspiration of forced breath,
No, nor the fruitful river in the eye,
Nor the dejected haviour of the visage,
Together with all forms, moods, shows of grief,
That can denote me truly. These indeed "seem,"
For they are actions that a man might play;
But I have that within which passeth show—
These but the trappings and the suits of woe.   (1.2.74–86)

Though Hamlet's use of the conventional Elizabethan forms of
mourning expresses his hostility to an unfeeling court, he is at
the same time speaking deeply of an experience that everyone
who has lost someone close to him must recognize. He is speaking of the early stages of grief, of its shock, of its inner and still
hidden sense of loss, and trying to describe what is not fully
describable—the literally inexpressible wound whose immediate
consequence is the dislocation, if not transvaluation, of our customary perceptions and feelings and attachments to life. The
loss of someone we love creates, in Jacques Lacan's phrase, "a hole
in the real," [6] and it is no accident that this speech sets in motion
Hamlet's preoccupation with seeming and being, including the
train of images of acting that is crystallized in the play within
the play. The peculiar centripetal pull of anger and sorrow that
the speech depicts remains as the central undercurrent of that

preoccupation, most notably in Hamlet's later soliloquy about the player's imitation of Hecuba's grief:

> Is it not monstrous that this player here,
> But in a fiction, in a dream of passion,
> Could force his soul so to his own conceit
> That from her working all his visage wanned,
> Tears in his eyes, distraction in 's aspect,
> A broken voice, and his whole function suiting
> With forms to his conceit? And all for nothing.
> For Hecuba!
> What's Hecuba to him, or he to Hecuba,
> That he should weep for her? What would he do
> Had he the motive and the cue for passion
> That I have?   (2.2.552–63)

Hamlet then goes on to rebuke himself for his own inaction, but the player's imitation of grief nonetheless moves him internally, as nothing else can, in fact to take action, as he conceives of the idea of staging a play to test both the ghost and the conscience of the King.

After Hamlet finishes answering his mother in the earlier court scene, the King offers his own consolation for Hamlet's grief:

> 'Tis sweet and commendable in your nature, Hamlet,
> To give these mourning duties to your father;
> But you must know your father lost a father;
> That father lost, lost his; and the survivor bound
> In filial obligation for some term
> To do obsequious sorrow. But to persever
> In obstinate condolement is a course
> Of impious stubbornness, 'tis unmanly grief,
> It shows a will most incorrect to heaven,
> A heart unfortified, a mind impatient,
> An understanding simple and unschooled;
> For what we know must be, and is as common
> As any the most vulgar thing to sense,

Why should we in our peevish opposition
Take it to heart? Fie, 'tis a fault to heaven,
A fault against the dead, a fault to nature,
To reason most absurd, whose common theme
Is death of fathers, and who still hath cried
From the first corpse till he that died today,
"This must be so."   (1.2.87–106)

There is in fact much in this consolation of philosophy which is
spiritually sound, and to which every human being must eventually accommodate himself, but it comes at the wrong time,
from the wrong person, and in its essential belittlement of the
heartache of grief, it comes with the wrong inflection. It is a
dispiriting irony of scholarship on this play that so many critics
should essentially take such words, from such a king, as a text for
their own indictments of Hamlet behavior. What a person who is
grieving needs, of course, is not the consolation of words, even
words that are true, but sympathy—and this Hamlet does not
receive, not from the court, not from his uncle, and more important, not from his own mother, to whom his grief over his father's
death is alien and unwelcome.

  After the King and Queen leave the stage, it is to his mother's lack of sympathy not only for him but for her dead husband
that Hamlet turns in particular pain:

O that this too too solid flesh would melt,
Thaw, and resolve itself into a dew,
Or that the Everlasting had not fixed
His canon 'gainst self-slaughter! O God, O God,
How weary, stale, flat, and unprofitable
Seem to me all the uses of this world!
Fie on't, ah fie! 'Tis an unweeded garden
That grows to seed; things rank and gross in nature
Possess it merely. That it should come to this—
But two months dead—nay, not so much, not two—
So excellent a king, that was to this
Hyperion to a satyr, so loving to my mother
That he might not beteem the winds of heaven

Visit her face too roughly! Heaven and earth,
Must I remember? Why, she would hang on him
As if increase of appetite had grown
By what it fed on, and yet within a month—
Let me not think on't; frailty, they name is woman—
A little month, or ere those shoes were old
With which she followed my poor father's body,
Like Niobe, all tears, why she, even she—
O God, a beast that wants discourse of reason
Would have mourned longer!—married with mine uncle,
My father's brother, but no more like my father
Than I to Hercules; within a month,
Ere yet the salt of most unrighteous tears
Had left the flushing of her gallèd eyes,
She married. O most wicked speed, to post
With such dexterity to incestuous sheets!
It is not, nor it cannot come to good.
But break, my heart, for I must hold my tongue. (1.2.129–58)

This is an exceptionally suggestive speech and the first of many that seem to invite oedipal interpretations of the play. About these I do not propose to speak directly, except to remark that the source of Hamlet's so-called oedipal anxiety is real and present, it is not an archaic and repressed fantasy. Hamlet does perhaps protest too much, in this soliloquy and elsewhere, about his father's superiority to his uncle (and to himself), and throughout the play he is clearly preoccupied with his mother's sexual appetite; but these ambivalences and preoccupations, whatever their unconscious roots, are elicited by a situation, palpable and external to him, in which they are acted out. The oedipal configurations of Hamlet's predicament, in other words, inhabit the whole world of the play, they are not simply a function of his characterization, even though they resonate with it profoundly.[7] There is every reason, in reality, for a son to be deeply troubled and discomposed by the appetite of a mother who betrays his father's memory by her incestuous marriage,[8] within a month, to his brother, and murderer, and there is surely more than reason for a son to be obsessed for a time with a father who literally returns from the grave to haunt him. But in any case, I think that at least early in the play, if not also later, such oedipal echoes cannot be disentangled from Hamlet's grief, and Shakespeare's purpose in arousing them is not to call Hamlet's character to judgment, but to expand our understanding of the nature and intensity of his suffering. For all these resonant events come upon Hamlet while he has still not even begun to assimilate the loss of a living father, while he is still mourning, seemingly alone in Denmark, for the death of a king, and their major psychic impact and importance, I think, is that they protract and vastly dilate the process of his grief.

Freud called this process the work of mourning and described it in his essay "Mourning and Melancholia" in a way that seems exceptionally germane to this play. Almost all of Freud's ideas can also be found in some form in the vast Renaissance literature on melancholy,[9] but Freud's discussion perhaps best suggests the coherence they had in Shakespeare's imagination.[10] The major preoccupation of the essay is, in fact, the pathology of melancholy, or what we would now more commonly call depression, but in the course of his discussion Freud finds unusually suggestive analogies and distinctions between mourning and melancholy. He points out, to begin with, that except in one respect the characteristics of normal grief and of pathological depression are the same, and that the two states can easily be confused—as they are, endemically, in interpretations of Hamlet's character. The characteristics of depression, Freud observes, are deep and painful dejection, a loss of interest in the outside world, an inability to act, and self-disgust as well as self-reproach. Except for the loss of faith in oneself, Freud continues, "the same traits are met with in grief": "Profound mourning, the reaction to the loss of a loved person, contains the same feeling of pain, loss of interest in the outside world—in so far as it does not recall the dead one—loss of capacity to adopt any new object of love, which would mean a replacing of the one mourned, the same turning from every active effort that is not connected with thoughts of the dead." Freud remarks that "though grief involves grave departures from the normal attitude of life, it never occurs to us to regard it as a morbid condition. We rest assured that after a lapse of time it will be overcome, and we look upon any interference with it as inadvisable or even harmful." [11]

The process by which grief is overcome, the work of mourning, Freud describes as a struggle—the struggle between the instinctive human disposition to remain libidinally bound to the dead person and the necessity to acknowledge the clear reality of his loss. "The task," he writes, is "carried through bit by bit," at enormous expense of time and energy, "while all the time the existence of the lost object is continued in the mind." "Each single one of the memories and hopes which bound the libido to the object" must be "brought up" and relinquished. "Why this process" Freud adds, "of carrying out the behest of reality bit by bit, which is in the nature of a compromise, should be so extraordinarily painful is not at all easy to explain in terms of mental economics. It is worth noting that this pain seems natural to us." [12]

Freud's wonderment at the pain of grief must seem odd to most of us, and it may be a function of his general unwillingness in most of his writing, including *Beyond the Pleasure Principle*, to deal directly with death itself. The issue is important because it is related to an astonishing lapse in the argument of "Mourning and Melancholia," which is critical to an understanding of *Hamlet*, and which might have helped Freud himself account for the extraordinary pain of grief in terms of his own conception of mental economics. For what Freud leaves out in his consideration of mourning is its normal but enormously disturbing component of protest and anger—initially anger at being wounded and abandoned, but fundamentally a protest, both conscious and unconscious, against the inescapably mortal condition of human life.

Freud finds such anger in depression, and with his analysis of that state few would wish to quarrel. The salient points of his argument are that in depression there is "an unconscious loss of a love-object, in contradistinction to mourning, in which there is nothing unconscious about the loss," and that there is a fall of self-esteem and a consistent cadence of self-reproach which is also not found in mourning. The key to an understanding of this condition, Freud continues, is the perception that the self-criticism of depression is really anger turned inwards, "that the self-reproaches are reproaches against a loved object which have been shifted onto the patient's own ego." The "complaints" of depressed people, he remarks, "are really 'plaints' in the legal sense of the word ... everything derogatory that they say of themselves relates at bottom to someone else." All the actions of a depressed person, Freud concludes, "proceed from an attitude of revolt, a mental constellation which by a certain process has become transformed into melancholic contrition." [13] Freud's explanation of the dynamics of this process is involved and technical, but there are two major points that emerge clearly and are highly relevant to *Hamlet*. The first is that there is, in a depressed person, "an *identification* of the ego with the abandoned object." "The shadow of the object," he says, "falls upon the ego," so that the ego can "henceforth be criticized by a special mental faculty like an object, like the forsaken object. In this way the loss of the object becomes transformed into a loss in the ego." [14] The second point that Freud stresses is that because there is an ambivalent relation to the lost object to begin with, the regressive movement toward identification is also accompanied by a regressive movement toward sadism, a movement whose logical culmination is suicide, the killing in the self of the lost object with whom the depressed person has so thoroughly identified. Freud adds that in only one other situation in human life is the ego so overwhelmed by the object, and that is in the state of intense love.

With these analogies and distinctions in mind, let us now return to the opening scene at court. As has already been suggested, in his first speech to his mother, "Seems, madam? Nay, it *is.* I know not 'seems,' " Hamlet speaks from the very heart of grief of the supervening reality of his loss and of its inward wound, and the accent of normal, if intense, grief remains dominant in his subsequent soliloquy as well. It is true that in that soliloquy his mind turns to thoughts of "self-slaughter," but those thoughts notwithstanding, the emphasis of the speech is not one of self-reproach. It is not himself, but the uses of the world that Hamlet finds "weary, stale, flat, and unprofitable," and his mother's frailty suggests a rankness and grossness in nature itself. The "plaints" against his mother that occupy the majority of his speech are conscious and both his anger and ambivalence toward her fully justified. Even on the face of it, her hasty remarriage makes a mockery of his father's memory that intensifies the real pain and loneliness of his loss; and if he also feels his own ego threatened, and if there is a deeper cadence of grief in his words, it is because he is already beginning to sense that the shadow of a crime with "the primal eldest curse upon't" (3.3.37) has fallen upon him, a crime that is not delusional and not his, and that eventually inflicts a punishment upon him that tries his spirit and destroys his life. The last lines of Hamlet's soliloquy are: "It is not, nor it cannot come to good. / But break, my heart, for I must hold my tongue." These lines show Hamlet's prescience, not his disease, and the instant he completes them Horatio, Marcellus, and Barnardo enter to tell him of the apparition of his dead father, the ghost that is haunting the kingdom and has been a part of our own consciousness from the very outset of the play.

Hamlet's subsequent meeting with the ghost of his father is both the structural and psychic nexus of the play. The scene is so familiar to us that the extraordinary nature of its impact on Hamlet can be overlooked, even in the theater. It begins with Hamlet expressing pity for the ghost and the ghost insisting that he attend to a more "serious" purpose:

> *Ghost*   List, Hamlet, list, O list!
>   If thou didst ever thy dear father love—
> *Hamlet*   O God!
> *Ghost*   Revenge his foul and most unnatural murder.
>
> (1.5.22–25)

The ghost then confirms to Hamlet's prophetic soul that "The serpent that did sting they father's life / Now wears his crown," and he proceeds to describe both Gertrude's remarriage and his own murder in his orchard in terms that seem deliberately to evoke echoes of the serpent in the Garden of Eden. The ghost ends his recital saying,

> O, horrible, O horrible, most horrible!
> If thou has nature in thee, bear it not.

Let not the royal bed of Denmark be
A couch for luxury and damnèd incest.
But howsoever thou pursuest this act,
Taint not thy mind, not let thy soul contrive
Against thy mother aught. Leave her to heaven,
And to those thorns that in her bosom lodge
To prick and sting her. Fare thee well at once.
The glow-worm shows the matin to be near,
And gins to pale his uneffectual fire.
Adieu, adieu, Hamlet. Remember me.   *Exit*

(1.5.39–40, 80–91)

Hamlet's answering speech, as the ghost exits, is profound, and it predicates the state of his mind and feeling until the beginning of the last act of the play:

O all you host of heaven! O earth! What else?
And shall I couple hell? O fie! Hold, hold, my heart,
And you, my sinews, grow not instant old,
But bear me stiffly up. Remember thee?
Ay, thou poor ghost, while memory holds a seat
In this distracted globe. Remember thee?
Yea, from the table of my memory
I'll wipe away all trivial fond records,
All saws of books, all forms, all pressures past,
That youth and observation copied there,
And thy commandment all alone shall live
Within the book and volume of my brain
Unmixed with baser matter. Yes, yes, by heaven.
O most pernicious woman!
O villain, villain, smiling, damnèd villain!
My tables,
My tables—meet it is I set it down
That one may smile and smile and be a villain!
At least I am sure it may be so in Denmark.
    He writes
So, uncle, there you are. Now to my word:

It is "Adieu, adieu, remember me."
I have sworn't. (1.5.92–114)

This is a crucial and dreadful vow for many reasons, but the most important, as Freud places us in a position to understand, is that the ghost's injunction to remember him, an injunction that Shakespeare's commitment to the whole force of the revenge genre never really permits either us or Hamlet to question, brutally intensifies Hamlet's mourning and makes him incorporate in its work what we would normally regard as the pathology of depression. For as we have seen, the essence of the work of mourning is the internal process by which the ego heals its wound, differentiates itself from the object, and slowly, bit by bit, cuts its libidinal ties with the one who has died. Yet this is precisely what the ghost forbids, and forbids, moreover, with a lack of sympathy for Hamlet's grief that is even more pronounced than the Queen's. He instead tells Hamlet that if ever he loved his father, he should remember him; he tells Hamlet of Gertrude's incestuous remarriage in a way that makes her desire, if not the libido itself, seem inseparable from murder and death; and finally he tells Hamlet to kill. Drawing upon and crystallizing the deepest energies of the revenge-play genre, the ghost thus enjoins Hamlet to identify with him in his sorrow and to give murderous purpose to his anger. He consciously compels in Hamlet, in other words, the regressive movement toward identification and sadism that together usually constitute the unconscious dynamics of depression. It is only after this scene that Hamlet feels punished with what he later calls a "sore distraction" (5.2.176) and he begins to reproach himself for his own nature and to meditate on suicide. The ghost, moreover, not only compels this process in Hamlet, like much of the world of the play, he incarnates it. The effect of his appearance and behest to Hamlet is to literalize Hamlet's subsequent movement toward the realm of death which he inhabits, and away from all of the bonds that nourish life and make it desirable, away from "all trivial fond records, / All saws of books, all forms, all pressures past." As C. S. Lewis insisted long ago, the ghost leads Hamlet into a spiritual and psychic region that seems poised between the living and the dead.[15] It is significant that Hamlet is subsequently described in images that suggest the ghost's countenance[16] and significant too, as we shall see later, that Hamlet's own appearance and state of mind change, at the beginning of act 5, at the moment when it is possible to say that he has finally come to terms with the ghost and with his father's death and has completed the work of mourning.

Shakespeare intends us always to retain a sense of intensified mourning rather than of disease in Hamlet, partly because Hamlet is always conscious of the manic roles he plays and is always lucid with Horatio, but also because his thoughts and feelings turn outward as well as inward and his behavior is finally a symbiotic response to the actually diseased world of the play. And though that diseased world, poisoned at the root by a truly guilty king, eventually represents an overwhelming tangle of guilt, its main emphasis, both for Hamlet and for us, is the experience of grief. The essential focus of the action as well as the source of its consistent pulsations of feeling, the pulsations which continuously charge both Hamlet's sorrow and his anger (and in which the whole issue of delay is subsumed) is the actuality of conscious, not unconscious, loss. For in addition to the death of his father in this play, Hamlet suffers the loss amounting to death of all those persons, except Horatio, whom he has most loved and who have most animated and given meaning to his life. He loses his mother, he loses Ophelia, and he loses his friends; and we can have no question that these losses are real and inescapable.

The loss of his mother is the most intense and the hardest to discuss. One should perhaps leave her to heaven as the ghost says, but even he cannot follow that advice. Hamlet is genuinely betrayed by her, most directly by her lack of sympathy for him. She is clearly sexually drawn and loyal to her new husband, and she is said to live almost by Hamlet's looks, but she is nonetheless essentially inert, oblivious to the whole realm of experience through which her son travels. She seems not to care, and seems particularly not to care about his grief. Early in the play, when Claudius and others are in hectic search of the reason for Hamlet's melancholy, she says with bovine imperturbability, "I doubt it is no other but the main—/ His father's death and our o'er-hasty marriage" (2.2.56–57). That over-hasty and incestuous marriage, which, as Roland M. Frye has amply documented, would have been even more scandalous to Elizabethan sensibilities than it is to ours, creates a reservoir of literally grievous anger in Hamlet.[17] It suggests to him the impermanence upon which the Player King later insists (3.2.185–92), and it also, less obviously, compels Hamlet to think of the violation of the union that gave him his own life and being. It is very difficult, under any circumstances, to think precisely upon our parents and their relationship without causing deep tremors in our selves, and for Hamlet the circumstances are extraordinary. In addition marriage has a sacramental meaning to him that has been largely lost in modern society. Like the ghost, Hamlet always speaks reverently of the sanctity of marriage vows, and the one occasion on which he mocks marriage is in fact an attack upon Claudius's presumption to have replaced his father. As he is leaving for England, Hamlet addresses Claudius and says, "Farewell, dear mother." Claudius says, "Thy loving father, Hamlet," and Hamlet answers, "My mother. Father and mother is man and wife, man and wife is one flesh, and so my mother" (4.3.51–54). Behind the scriptural image in this ferocious attack upon Claudius is both Hamlet's memory of his father's true marriage with his mother, a memory that has an almost prelapsarian resonance, and a visualization of the concupiscence through which his mother has defiled that sacrament and made Claudius's guilt a part of her own being. This same adulterated image of matrimony lies behind his intense reproaches both against himself and Ophelia in the speech in which he urges Ophelia to go to a nunnery: "Get thee to a nunnery. Why wouldst thou be a breeder of sinners? I am myself indifferent honest, but yet I could accuse me of such things that it were better my mother had not borne me. I am very proud, revengeful, ambitious, with more offences at my beck than I have thoughts to put them in, imagination to give them shape, or time to act them in. What should such fellows as I do crawling between heaven and earth?" (3.1.123–31).

Some of Hamlet's anger against Ophelia spills over, as it does in this speech, from his rage against his mother, but Ophelia herself gives him cause. There is no reason to doubt her own word, at the beginning of the play, that Hamlet has importuned her "with love / In honorable fashion ... And hath given countenance to his speech ... With all the holy vows of heaven" (1.3.110–11, 113–14); and there is certainly no reason to question his own passionate declaration at the end of the play, over her grave, that he loved her deeply:

> I loved Ophelia. Forty thousand brothers
> Could not, with all their quantity of love,
> Make up my sum.   (5.1.267–69)

Both Hamlet's grief and his task constrain him from realizing this love, but Ophelia's own behavior clearly intensifies his frustration and anguish. By keeping the worldly and disbelieving advice of her brother and father as "watchman" to her "heart" (1.3.46), she denies the heart's affection not only in Hamlet but in herself; and both denials add immeasurably to Hamlet's sense of loneliness and loss—and anger. Her rejection of him echoes his mother's inconstancy and denies him the possibility even of imagining the experience of loving and being loved by a woman at a time when he obviously needs such love most profoundly; and her rejection of her own heart reminds him of the evil court whose shadow, he accurately senses, has fallen upon her and directly threatens him. Most of Hamlet's speeches to Ophelia condense all of these feelings. They are spoken from a sense of suppressed as well as rejected love, for the ligaments between him and Ophelia are very deep in the play. It is she who first reports on his melancholy transformation,

> with a look so piteous in purport
> As if he had been loosèd out of hell
> To speak of horrors.   (2.1.83–85)

It is she who remains most acutely conscious of the nobility of mind and form that has, she says, been "blasted with ecstasy"

(3.1.163); and it is she, after Hamlet has gone to England, who most painfully takes up his role and absorbs his grief to the point of real madness and suicide. It is no accident that her funeral should decisively crystallize his own preparedness for death.

Rosencrantz and Guildenstern are less close to Hamlet's heart, and because they are such unequivocal sponges of the King, he can release his anger against them without any ambivalence, but at least initially they too amplify both his and our sense of the increasing emptiness of his world. We are so accustomed to treating Rosencrantz and Guildenstern as vaguely comic twins that we can forget the great warmth with which Hamlet first welcomes them to Denmark and the urgency and openness of his pleas for the continuation of their friendship. "I will not sort you with the rest of my servants," he says to them,

> for, to speak to you like an honest man, I am most dreadfully attended. But in the beaten way of friendship, what make you at Elsinore?
> *Rosencrantz* To visit you, my lord, no other occasion.
> *Hamlet* Beggar that I am, I am even poor in thanks, but I thank you; and sure, dear friends, my thanks are too dear a halfpenny. Were you not sent for? Is it your own inclining? Is it a free visitation? Come, deal justly with me. Come, come. Nay, speak.
> *Guildenstern* What would we say, my lord?
> *Hamlet* Why, anything—but to th' purpose. You were sent for, and there is a kind of confession in your looks which your modesties have not craft enough to colour. I know the good King and Queen have sent for you.
> *Rosencrantz* To what end, my lord?
> *Hamlet* That you must teach me. But let me conjure you by the rights of our fellowship, by the consonancy of our youth, by the obligation of our everpreserved love, and by what more dear a better proposer could charge you withal, be even and direct with me whether you were sent for or no.
>
> (2.2.268–89)

Rosencrantz and Guildenstern, of course, cannot be direct with him, and Hamlet cuts his losses with them quite quickly and eventually quite savagely. But it is perhaps no accident that immediately following this exchange, when he must be fully realizing the extent to which, except for Horatio, he is now utterly alone in Denmark with his grief and his task, he gives that grief a voice that includes in its deep sadness and its sympathetic imagination a conspectus of Renaissance thought about the human condition. "I have of late," he tells his former friends,

> —but wherefore I know not—lost all my mirth, forgone all custom of exercise; and indeed it goes so heavily with my disposition that this goodly frame, the earth, seems to me a sterile promontory. This most excellent canopy the air, look you, this brave o'erhanging, this majestical roof fretted with golden fire—why, it appeareth no other thing to me than a foul and pestilent congregation of vapours. What a piece of work is man! How noble in reason, how infinite in faculty, in form and moving how express and admirable, in action how like an angel, in apprehension how like a god—the beauty of the world, the paragon of animals! And yet to me what is this quintessence of dust?   (2.2.296–309)

"In grief," Freud remarks in "Mourning and Melancholia," "the world becomes poor and empty; in melancholia it is the ego itself." [18] During most of the action of *Hamlet* we cannot make this distinction. For the first four acts of the play, the world in which Hamlet must exist and act is characterized in all its parts not merely as diseased, but specifically for Hamlet as one that is being emptied of all the human relationships that nourish the ego and give it purpose and vitality. It is a world that is essentially defined—generically, psychically, spiritually—by a ghost whose very countenance, "more / In sorrow than in anger" (1.2.228–29), binds Hamlet to a course of grief that is deeper and wider than any in our literature. It is a world of mourning.

At the beginning of act 5, when Hamlet returns from England, that world seems to change, and Hamlet with it. Neither the countenance of the ghost nor his tormented and tormenting spirit seems any longer to be present in the play, and Hamlet begins to alter in state of mind as he already has in his dress. He stands in the graveyard that visually epitomizes the play's preoccupation with death, a scene that the clowns insistently associate with Adam's sin and Hamlet himself with Cain's, and he contemplates the skull of the man who carried him on his back when he was a small child. The scene resonates with the *memento mori* tradition that has intensified as well as enlarged his suffering from the first:

> Alas, poor Yorick. I knew him, Horatio—a fellow of infinite jest, of most excellent fancy. He hath borne me on his back a thousand times; and now, how abhorred my imagination is! My gorge rises at it. Here hung those lips that I have kissed I know not how oft. Where be your gibes now, your gambols, your songs, your flashes of merriment that were wont to set the table on a roar? Not one now to mock your own grinning? Quite chop-fallen? Now get you to my lady's chamber and tell her, let her paint an inch thick, to this favour she must come. Make her laugh at that. (5.1.180–90)

This speech suggests the underlying context for Hamlet's earlier attacks not only upon the vanity of his mother and Ophelia but also upon the vanity of all human existence.[19] But his mood now has begun to shift. There is a characteristic inflection of pain and protest in his invocation of an intellectual tradition that was originally designed to promote resignation, and there is a suggestion too, by Horatio, that he is still considering death "too curiously" (5.1.201), but there is no longer the sense that he and his world are conflated in the convulsive activity of grief. That activity seems to be drawing to a close, and his own sense of differentiation is decisively crystallized when, at the end of the scene, in a moment reminiscent of the one in which he reacts to the imitation of Hecuba's grief, he responds to Laertes's enactment of a grief that seems a parody of his own:

What is he whose grief
Bears such an emphasis, whose phrase of sorrow
Conjures the wand'ring stars and makes them stand
Like wonder-wounded hearers? This is I,
Hamlet the Dane.   (5.1.251–55)

It is an especially painful but inescapable paradox of Hamlet's tragedy that the final ending of his grief and the liberation of his self should be coextensive with the apprehension of his own death. After agreeing to the duel with Laertes that he is confident of winning, he nevertheless tells Horatio of his premonition of death, "But thou wouldst not think how all here about my heart—but it is no matter" (5.2.158–59); and when Horatio urges him to postpone the duel, he says, in the famous speech that signifies, if it does not explain, the decisive change of his spirit: "Not a whit. We defy augury. There's a special providence in the fall of a sparrow. If it be now, 'tis not to come. If it be not to come, it will be now. If it be not now, yet it will come. The readiness is all. Since no man has aught of what he leaves, what is't to leave betimes?" (5.2.165–70). The theological import of these lines, with their luminous reference to Matthew, has long been recognized, but the particular emphasis upon death suggests a psychological coordinate. For what makes Hamlet's acceptance of Providence finally intelligible and credible to us emotionally, what confirms the truth of it to our own experience, is our sense, as well as his, that the great anguish and struggle of his grief are over, and that he has completed the work of mourning. He speaks to Horatio quietly, almost serenely, with an unexultant calm that characterizes the end of the long, inner struggle of grief. He has looked at the face of death in his father's ghost, he has endured death and loss in all the human beings he has loved, and he now accepts those losses as an inevitable part of his own condition. "The readiness is all" suggests the crystallization of his awareness of the larger dimension of time that has enveloped his tragedy from the start, including the revenge drama of Fortinbras's grievances on the outskirts of the action and that of the appalling griefs of Polonius's family deep inside it,[20] but the line also most specifically states what is perhaps the last and most difficult task of mourning, his own readiness to die.

The ending of Hamlet's mourning is finally mysterious in the play, as the end of mourning usually is in actual life, but it is made at least partially explicable by the very transfusion of energy between him and the other characters that constitutes his grief to begin with. Early in the play he seems to absorb into himself the whole body of the world's sorrow and protest, as later in the play he seems to expel it. The ghost, I think, he partly exorcises and partly incorporates. He increasingly gives expression to much of its vengeful anger—most definitively, perhaps, when he uses his father's signet to hoist Rosencrantz and Guildenstern on their own petard—but at the same time he thereby eventually frees himself to internalize the "radiance" of his father's memory rather than the ghost's shadow of it.[21] His mother herself cannot really be transformed, but he makes her feel the force of his grief even if she cannot understand it, and in the closet scene at least, he succeeds in transferring some of the pain in his own heart to hers. To Claudius he transfers a good deal more. By means of the play within the play, including his own interpolated lines on mutability, Hamlet at once acts out the deep anger and sorrow of his grief and transmits the fever of their energy to the guilty King in whose blood he thereafter rages "like the hectic" (4.3.68).[22] But perhaps most important, not so much in effecting Hamlet's recovery as in representing its inner dynamics and persuading us of its authenticity, are the transformations that Ophelia and Laertes undergo during the period Hamlet himself is offstage on his voyage to England. Ophelia, as we have seen, drains off Hamlet's incipient madness and suicidal imaginings into her own "weeping brook" (4.7.147) of grief, and she begins to do so precisely at the moment Hamlet leaves the stage for England. She enters *"mad, [her hair down, with a lute]"* (4.5.20), singing songs which signify not only the consuming pain of the loss of her father but also the self-destructive sexual frustration that has afflicted Hamlet as well as her. At almost the same moment, Laertes enters the stage, and while Hamlet himself later explicitly sees in Laertes's predicament an analogue of his own, Laertes's sorrow and anger are quickly corrupted; and his poisonous allegiance with the King simultaneously dramatizes the most destructive vengeful energies of grief and seems to draw those energies away from Hamlet and into himself. This whole movement of energy between Hamlet and the other characters suggests the symbiotic relation between the protagonists and the secondary characters in the medieval morality drama as well as the unconscious processes of condensation and displacement that are represented in dreams, and its result is our profound sense at the end of the play that Hamlet's self has been reconstituted as well as recovered. That sense is especially clear in act 5 in Hamlet's own entirely conscious and generous relation to Laertes, the double who threatens his life but not his identity, who presents an "image" of his "cause" (5.2.78), but never of the untainted heroic integrity of his grief.

Hamlet's generosity to Laertes at the end of the play is especially significant, I think, because it brings to the surface the underlying inflection of charity that makes Hamlet's whole experience of grief so humane and so remote from the moral or psychological pathology for which many critics, including Freud himself, indict him. In the only mention he makes of *Hamlet* in "Mourning and Melancholia," Freud remarks that the melancholiac often has access to exceptionally deep insights and that his self-criticism can come "very near to self-knowledge; we can only wonder why a man must become ill before he can discover truth of this kind. For there can be no doubt that whoever holds and expresses to others such an opinion of himself—one that Hamlet harboured of himself and all men—that man is ill, whether he speaks the truth or is more or less unfair to himself."[23] In a footnote Freud cites as evidence of Hamlet's misanthropy and sickness his criticism of Polonius: "Use every man after his desert, and who should scape whipping?" (2.2.531–32). What Freud misses, of course, and it is to miss much, is not only that Hamlet becomes all men in his grief, but that he does so in the image of charity that the very line evokes. For the premise of Hamlet's statement, like Portia's in *The Merchant of Venice*, is "That in the course of justice none of us / Should see salvation," and that therefore

we do pray for mercy,
And that same prayer doth teach us all to render
The deeds of mercy.   (4.1.196–99)

Hamlet's line, to be sure, does not have this explicit emphasis, but in its context there is no question that the motive of his statement is to have Polonius use the players kindly and that the ultimate burden of his thought is, like Portia's, the verse, "Forgive us our trespasses as we forgive those who trespass against us." If the great anger and sorrow of Hamlet's grief makes his own experience of these trespasses tragically acute and painful, the same combination of feelings eventually expands his capacity to understand, if not forgive, them.

I think this generosity and integrity of grief lie close to the heart both of Hamlet's mystery and the play's. *Hamlet* is an immensely complicated tragedy, and anything one says about it leaves one haunted by what has not been said. But precisely in a play whose suggestiveness has no end, it seems especially important to remember what actually happens. Hamlet himself is sometimes most preoccupied with delay, and with the whole attendant metaphysical issue of the relation between thought and action, but as his own experience shows, there is finally no action that can be commensurate with grief, not even the killing of a guilty king, and it is Hamlet's experience of grief, and his recovery from it, to which we ourselves respond most deeply. He is a young man who comes home from his university to find his father dead and his mother remarried to his father's murderer. Subsequently the woman he loves rejects him, he is betrayed by his friends, and finally and most painfully, he is betrayed by a mother whose mutability seems to strike at the heart of human affection. In the midst of these waves of losses, which seem themselves to correspond to the spasms of grief, he is visited by the ghost of his father, who places upon him a proof of love and a task of vengeance that he cannot refuse without denying his own being. The ghost draws upon the emotional taproot of the revenge-play genre and dilates the natural sorrow and anger of Hamlet's multiple griefs until they include all human frailty in their protest and sympathy and touch upon the deepest synapses of grief in our own lives, not only for those who have died, but for those, like ourselves, who are still alive.

CHAPTER III

OTHELLO

OTHELLO IS COMPOSED of an extraordinary mixture of anti-
thetical states of feeling and being. The extremes are literally as well as emblematically represented in Desdemona and
Iago, but they are most deeply incarnated in Othello himself,
who moves from one to the other, from the love celebrated in
the first half of the play to the nearly utter disintegration and
destruction dramatized in the second half. The contrast is so
drastic that even critics sympathetic to Othello can find it insupportable. *Othello* is not the only Shakespearean tragedy to
dramatize such oppositions—all of the major tragedies move essentially and starkly from life to death—but *Othello* poses a peculiar difficulty for critics because its preoccupations are so
unremittingly sexual. At the core of *Othello* is an uncomfortably
intense focus upon the sexual relationship between a man and a
woman in marriage, a relationship that was as inherently paradoxical and mysterious to Elizabethans as it is to us. It is a mystery celebrated in many of the Petrarchan conceits that *Othello*
literally enacts,[1] but its essential paradox is most explicitly and
profoundly described in the words of St. Paul that are cited in
the marriage liturgy: "So men are bound to love their own wives
as their own bodies. He that loveth his own wife, loveth himself.
For never did any man hate his own flesh, but nourisheth it and
cherisheth it, even as the Lord doth the Congregation: for we are

members of his body, of his flesh and of his bones. For this cause shall a man leave father and mother, and shall be joined unto his wife, and they two shall be one flesh. This mystery is great, but I speak of Christ and of the congregation."[2] Referring to the Bible, Freud describes the same mystery in approximately analogous terms: "A man shall leave father and mother—according to the Biblical precept—and shall cleave to his wife; then are tenderness and sensuality united." He explains that "to ensure a fully normal attitude in love," the union of both "currents" of feeling is necessary, and that this union is ultimately derived from a child's early symbiotic relationship with his mother in which his love for her and for himself are identical.[3] I think we should attend to both St. Paul and Freud in interpreting *Othello.*

In *Troilus and Cressida* Hector warns Troilus that it is "mad idolatry / To make the service greater than the god" (2.2.55–56), and that play in fact depicts a world in which madness and idolatry do characterize all social and sexual relationships. It is essential to recognize at the outset that the world of *Othello* is different, that Desdemona is not Helen or Cressida, that she is true, and that there is no service greater than she deserves. One would suppose these to be self-evident propositions, but there are notable critics who dispute them. A. P. Rossiter, for example, actually equates Desdemona with Helen, indicts Othello for ascribing "false excellences" to her, and dismisses her as a "pathetic, girlish, nearly-blank sheet."[4] W. H. Auden responds to her more fully, but thinks even worse of her. "Everybody must pity Desdemona," he writes,

> but I cannot bring myself to like her. Her determination to marry Othello—it was she who virtually did the proposing—seems the romantic crush of a silly schoolgirl rather than a mature affection; it is Othello's adventures, so unlike the civilian life she knows, which captivate her rather than Othello as a person. . . . her deception of her own father makes an unpleasant impression. . . . Before Cassio speaks to her, she has already discussed him with her husband and learned that he is to be reinstated as soon as is opportune. A sensible wife would have told

Cassio this and left matters alone. In continuing to badger Othello, she betrays a desire to prove to herself and to Cassio that she can make her husband do as she pleases. Her lie about the handkerchief is, in itself, a trivial fib but, had she really regarded her husband as her equal, she might have admitted the loss. . . . Though her relation with Cassio is perfectly innocent, one cannot but share Iago's doubts as to the durability of the marriage. It is worth noting that, in the willow-song scene with Emilia, she speaks with admiration of Ludovico and then turns to the topic of adultery. . . . Given a few more years of Othello and of Emilia's influence and she might well, one feels, have taken a lover.[5]

Auden's response is deeply perverse, but I have cited it at such length because in sophisticated or disguised form his assumptions and prejudices underlie more criticism of the play than might at first be apparent. Though I suppose few readers of *Othello*, and still fewer of its spectators, would even conceive of faulting Desdemona for not being "sensible," there are many who do feel that she is too good to be true, too innocent to be a wife or too wifely to be innocent, and this attitude is quite as damaging to the play as Auden's outright hostility. Either way, the play eventually starts turning inside out. It is therefore important to any interpretation to pay detailed attention to the terms in which Shakespeare presents Desdemona and not to take her for granted.

The first substantial impression we receive of her is in Othello's description of their courtship. He tells how he often visited her father's house, how he recounted the story of his life at Brabantio's request, and how he drew from Desdemona a "prayer of earnest heart" to tell that story to her:

> I did consent,
> And often did beguile her of her tears
> When I did speak of some distressful stroke
> That my youth suffered. My story being done,
> She gave me for my pains a world of kisses.

She swore in faith 'twas strange, 'twas passing strange,
'Twas pitiful, 'twas wondrous pitiful.
She wished she had not heard it, yet she wished
That heaven had made her such a man. She thankèd me,
And bade me, if I had a friend that loved her,
I should but teach him how to tell my story,
And that would woo her. Upon this hint I spake.
She loved me for the dangers I had passed,
And I loved her that she did pity them.   (1.3.151, 154–67)

The tenor of Othello's whole speech, as well as the Duke's reaction to it—"I think this tale would win my daughter, too" (1.3.170)—should alone suggest that Desdemona is hardly an overaggressive schoolgirl, that their wooing is delicately mutual, and that in responding to the "story" of his life she was responding to the man it revealed, since Othello truly "is what he has done."[6] But an even more important index of Desdemona's characterization is the description of the precise nature of her response. After centuries of sentimentalist thinking, we may be disposed to regard tears and the capacity for pity as cheap commodities, but Shakespeare did not. Pity is always exalted in the plays (the Italian word *pietà* may perhaps better suggest its Shakespearean connotations), and it is regularly the most compelling virtue of his heroines. It is incarnated in Cordelia when she returns to Britain, as she says, to "go about" her father's "business," weeping and praying:

All blest secrets,
All you unpublished virtues of the earth,
Spring with my tears, be aidant and remediate
In the good man's distress!   (4.3.24, 15–18)

It is inscribed in Miranda's characterization at the start of *The Tempest* when she laments to Prospero, "I have sufferèd / With those that I saw suffer," and he tells her to calm her "piteous heart" (1.2.5–6, 14). Desdemona's feeling for Othello is of this kind. It is a sign not that she is silly or guileful, but that she has a capacity to sympathize deeply with human suffering, that she has, as Prospero says of Miranda, "the very virtue of compassion" (1.2.27).

Desdemona enters immediately after Othello's speech and her father asks her, "Do you perceive in all this noble company / Where most you owe obedience?" The moment is charged both for those on stage and for us, and the impact and importance of her answer, the first words she speaks in the play, cannot be exaggerated:

> My noble father,
> I do perceive here a divided duty.
> To you I am bound for life and education.
> My life and education both do learn me
> How to respect you. You are the lord of duty,
> I am hitherto your daughter. But here's my husband,
> And so much duty as my mother showed
> To you, preferring you before her father,
> So much I challenge that I may profess
> Due to the Moor my lord.   (1.3.178–88)

These luminous lines, which are strongly reminiscent of those that Cordelia uses when she defies Lear (1.1.95–103), evoke the very cadence of the scriptural injunction to marry: "For this cause shall a man leave father and mother, and shall be joined unto his wife, and they two shall be one flesh"; and Desdemona's description of the transfer of her feelings from her father to her husband, with its invocation of her own mother as her example, touches in almost archetypal terms upon the psychological process by which a girl becomes a woman and a wife. These associations are unmistakable, and Desdemona's strikingly unusual choice of a husband only heightens their power. Othello's age, possibly the same as her father's, literalizes the psychological reverberations, and his blackness, as we shall see, intensifies the theological ones. It is nonsense to imagine that Shakespeare created such a speech for a character who was to be an unpleasant homiletic example, a "caution," as Thomas Rymer put it, "to all

Maidens of Quality how, without their Parents consent, they run away with Blackamoors."[7]

It is even greater nonsense to imagine that such a speech would introduce a girl incapable of "mature affection." As Desdemona immediately shows, she loves Othello as a wife should, body and soul. She insists on going with him to Cyprus in a speech that is even more remarkable for its spiritual and emotional poise than her first:

> That I did love the Moor to live with him,
> My downright violence and storm of fortunes
> May trumpet to the world. My heart's subdued
> Even to the very quality of my lord.
> I saw Othello's visage in his mind,
> And to his honours and his valiant parts
> Did I my soul and fortunes consecrate;
> So that, dear lords, if I be left behind,
> A moth of peace, and he go to the war,
> The rites for why I love him are bereft me,
> And I a heavy interim shall support
> By his dear absence. Let me go with him.   (1.3.248–59)

There are few instances in Shakespearean drama of so explicit, so natural, and so harmonious an integration of flesh and spirit. Sensuality and affection are inseparable in Desdemona's consciousness. She loves Othello to live with him; she acknowledges but is unashamed of the violence of her behavior; she wants to consummate the marriage; she is subdued to Othello's very quality ("utmost pleasure" in the quarto). At the same time, she consecrates her soul to his honor and valiancy, and says that she "saw Othello's visage in his mind." That charged and crucial statement cannot be fully appreciated apart from Othello's characterization, and we shall return to it, but for the moment we can at least observe that it testifies to a kind of spiritual "eyesight" that Shakespeare consistently celebrated in his other plays. The presence of this vision in Desdemona authenticates her desire for Othello and is an expression of the fullness as well as the transcendence of her love. It is also a measure of her own surpassing worth as an object of love.

Desdemona's subsequent appearances in the play only confirm and heighten these initial impressions of her love and of its value. In the scene of her arrival in Cyprus, Cassio refers to her as "the divine Desdemona" (2.1.74) and calls upon the men of Cyprus to kneel in adoration of her. At the same time he speaks of her in explicitly sexual terms:

> Great Jove, Othello guard,
> And swell his sail with thine own powerful breath,
> That he may bless this bay with his tall ship,
> Make love's quick pants in Desdemona's arms,
> Give renewed fire to our extincted spirits,
> And bring all Cyprus comfort.   (2.1.78–83)

That Cassio, as we later see, is incapable of unifying such idealized and sensual feelings in his own erotic life does not diminish the force of his perception of their union in Desdemona, and her sexual integrity is particularly radiant in this scene. In response to Othello's fear during their reunion that "not another comfort like to this / Succeeds in unknown fate," she says,

> The heavens forbid
> But that our loves and comforts should increase
> Even as our days do grow.   (2.1.193–96)

The pellucid beauty of these lines, as of so many others that Desdemona speaks, is a function of the harmony of instinctual and spiritual life Shakespeare represents in her, and it is characteristic that she should see the passage of time not as a threat to marriage but as a promise of its growth and fulfillment.

The promise, of course, is never fulfilled, and in the remainder of the play, as Iago pours his pestilence into Othello's ear, Desdemona becomes increasingly incapable not only of comforting her husband but even of understanding him. Many critics besides Auden interpret this failure as evidence of her own inadequacy. Whatever merit such a judgment might have in our lives outside the theater, in the world of the play it is the opposite of the truth, as Iago himself explicitly informs us:

> So I will turn her virtue into pitch,
> And out of her own goodness make the net
> That shall enmesh them all.   (2.3.351–53)

Iago is a liar, but not in his soliloquies, and Shakespeare gives us no reason to doubt him here. Quite the contrary, for our constant apprehension of how Desdemona's virtues are perverted is central to our response not only to her but to the entire action. She is human, she has a literal identity, and it is possible to see considerable stubbornness in her disastrous advocacy of Cassio, but to stage or read those scenes in which she pleads for Cassio as the exercises of a willful woman or a domineering wife is to misconstrue her motives and to become as subject to Iago's inversions as Othello does. Her fundamental concern is not for Cassio, for whom she does nevertheless feel affection, but for her husband, for Othello. She intuits, what we after all know, that Othello's alienation from Cassio is unnatural and injurious to them both. She sees Cassio as Othello's devoted friend,

> That came a-wooing with you, and so many a time
> When I have spoke of you dispraisingly
> Hath ta'en your part;   (3.3.72–74)

and she begs Othello to forgive him in the terms and for the reasons that truly prompt her:

> 'Tis as I should entreat you wear your gloves,
> Or feed on nourishing dishes, or keep you warm,
> Or sue to you to do a peculiar profit
> To your own person.   (3.3.78–81)

She is thinking, as ultimately she always does, of Othello, not of herself, and the conclusion of her plea is: "Be as your fancies teach you. / Whate'er you be, I am obedient" (3.3.89–90). And she is. She obeys Othello literally until death parts her from him.

She also continues, in the words of the liturgy, to love and honor him, and much of the horror and pity we experience at the end of the play comes from our perception of the ways in which her absolute fidelity to marriage helps destroy it. She misplaces the handkerchief in the first place because she cannot comprehend Othello's allusion to the pain in his forehead, and she uses it to bind his brow and to comfort him. It is he, in his distemper, who brushes it aside and "loses" it. The same innocence is the source of her persistence in pleading for Cassio while Othello asks her about the handkerchief, thus more deeply associating the two in his mind, and of her general incapacity to recognize and therefore cope with his jealousy. That innocence, as her wondering discussion of adultery with Emilia makes clear, is born of her own absolute marital chastity.[8] She may unconsciously apprehend more of what Emilia believes than she realizes, as her corruption of the willow-song seems to suggest,[9] and she is human enough, in mentioning Lodovico as a "proper man," to have intimations of a marriage that might have been better than her own, for she senses what is to come. She is also, certainly, momentarily terrified of dying (for which some critics, for some unfathomable reason, fault her), but her last words are for Othello, and her earlier bewilderment and fear only heighten our sense of the depth of her love, the monstrousness of its destruction, and the overwhelming pity of its loss. The worldly Emilia testifies, at the cost of her life, to the truth we ourselves most deeply feel: "Moor, she was chaste. She loved thee, cruel Moor" (5.2.256).

The peculiar integrity and power of Desdemona's characterization, as I have been suggesting throughout this discussion, are in part a function of the literalness of her exemplification of the religious and psychological commitments of marriage. As a result she is the most domestic of Shakespeare's heroines at the same time that she is one of the most elemental and numinous, and in the latter half of the play her symbolic overtones become particularly insistent. Othello compares her to a chrysolite, which was one of the twelve precious stones in the walls of the heavenly city (Rev. 21.20) and was traditionally associated with faith, constancy, and innocence, "all things in Christ";[10] and in his final speech, when he realizes how much he has lost, he speaks of her as a pearl, and his own image suggests the pearl of great price (Matt. 13.45–46).[11] Toward the end, a profusion of references associates her with heaven and salvation, and the more Othello sees and treats her as a devil, the more saintly she seems and becomes. In the worst of her suffering, as she kneels to Iago for help, she says:

> Unkindness may do much,
> And his unkindness may defeat my life,
> But never taint my love.   (4.2.163–65)

And she remains sacrificially true to that love as she dies:

> *Emilia*   O, who hath done this deed?
> *Desdemona*   Nobody, I myself. Farewell.
>   Commend me to my kind lord. O, farewell! (5.2.132–34)

It is this kind of love, with its manifold religious and psychological reverberations, its literal transcendence of death, to which Othello first responds and with which his own love resonates in the first two acts of the play. In these acts he and Desdemona are so well tuned that they seem together to be an elemental expression of that single state of being toward which marriage aspires, and his characterization cannot be understood apart from hers. His blackness and his age especially, his two most salient features, have enormous symbolic as well as literal significance in their marriage. In any performance his color and its contrast with Desdemona's are visually most powerful, and images of darkness and light permeate the language of the play. As G. K. Hunter has shown, there were two opposing conceptions of the black man in Elizabethan England.[12] The first was the primitive and ancient sense of black as the color of inferiority and wickedness, which was incorporated in early Christian eschatology and became deeply ingrained in Christian thinking. In

] 53 [

medieval and Renaissance drama and art, devils as well as evil men (the torturers of Christ, for instance) were commonly depicted as black. It is this sense of blackness that Shakespeare's audience would most likely have brought to the theater and that, with a particularly acrid emphasis upon sexual bestiality and unnaturalness, is strongly associated with Othello in the first few scenes of the play. The play opens with a cascade of obscene references to Othello's color and race—"thick-lips," "a Barbary horse," "the gross clasps of a lascivious Moor," "a gross revolt" (1.1.66, 113–14, 128, 136)—and Iago tells Brabantio explicitly that

> Even now, now, very now, an old black ram
> Is tupping your white ewe. Arise, arise!
> Awake the snorting citizens with the bell,
> Or else the devil will make a grandsire of you.   (1.1.88–91)

The "spiteful old pantaloon"[13] Brabantio himself picks up the litany.[13] He expresses disbelief that Desdemona could have "run from her guardage to the sooty bosom / Of such a thing as thou—to fear, not to delight," and repeatedly states that only pagan witchcraft, the "practices of cunning hell," can explain how "perfection so could err / Against all rules of nature" (1.2.71–72; 1.3.102, 100–101).

The other Elizabethan conception of blackness, more peculiar to Christian theology and less familiar now, was the notion that all men are black in their sinfulness, but become white in the knowledge of the Lord, a belief that was especially prevalent in evangelically tinted voyage literature, which treated inferior and black-faced foreigners as creatures whose innocence made them close to God and naturally prone to accept Christianity. The root metaphor of this attitude was drawn from the Song of Songs and the belief found expression as late as 1630 in a meditation by Bishop Hall "on the sight of a blackamoor":

> This is our colour spiritually; yet the eye of our gracious
> God and Savior, can see that beauty in us wherewith he
> is delighted. The true Moses marries a Blackamoor;

Christ, his church. It is not for us to regard the skin, but the soul. If that be innocent, pure, holy, the blots of an outside cannot set us off from the love of him who hath said, *Behold, thou are fair, my Sister, my Spouse:* if that be foul and black, it is not in the power of an angelical brightness of our hide, to make us other than a loathsome eye-sore to the Almighty.[14]

It is to this spiritual dynamic that Desdemona is clearly referring when she says, "I saw Othello's visage in his mind," and to which we ourselves are compelled to refer Othello once he comes on stage. His sense of command, of public decorum and courtesy, his dignity, and above all his remarkable devotion to Desdemona are instantly evident. The impression they make is all the more powerful, as Hunter and others have suggested, because Shakespeare has deliberately implicated us in the primordial prejudices of that other conception of the black man evoked in the discourse of Iago, Roderigo, and Brabantio in the first scene of the play.[15] We ourselves thus experience, we do not merely witness, the process of perception Desdemona describes. That process is kept constantly in our consciousness by Othello's literal appearance, by the pervasive imagery of blackness and fairness and of true and false vision, and by Iago's increasingly ominous and explicitly diabolic threats to turn the spiritual metaphor into an "ocular proof." Under these circumstances, and given the concurrent development of Desdemona as an incarnate ideal of marital love and of the charity that subsumes it, Othello's marked worship of her is an expression not, as so many critics would have it, of the intrinsic weakness of his love, but of its potential strength. Brabantio's last bitter words in the play are: "Look to her, Moor, if thou hast eyes to see. / She has deceived her father, and may thee." Othello answers, with the absolutism that characterizes him throughout, "My life upon her faith" (1.3.292–94). Iago is later to make deadly use of Brabantio's words, and when Othello immediately turns to "honest Iago" to care for Desdemona, we feel Othello's peril. His absolute commitment to Desdemona increases the peril, but it is not in itself idolatrous. His investment in Desdemona's vision of him, as opposed to her father's, is a precisely Christian choice, the very reverse of idolatry. It is a manifestation of the faith that in Elizabethan eyes was the deepest resource of the love that unites a man and woman in marriage.

The discrepancy between Othello's and Desdemona's age has much the same effect as his blackness in the early acts and is similarly related to the reverence that marks his love for her. As several critics have observed, the marriage of an old man and a young girl was traditional material for comedy or farce,[16] but Shakespeare again inverts his audience's expectations and thereby intensifies its response. Desdemona, as we have seen, is no May. She loves Othello body and soul, unreservedly, and neither at the beginning nor at the tragic end of the marriage is she ever untrue to the ideal of one flesh to which she has consecrated herself. Othello, similarly, in the beginning is no January. He is a general replete with power and respect, and unlike his comic prototypes, as Shakespeare takes pains to establish, he is neither lascivious nor impotent. In a much misunderstood speech to the Duke and Venetian lords, he seconds Desdemona's request to accompany him to Cyprus, "not," as he says,

> To please the palate of my appetite,
> Nor to comply with heat—the young affects
> In me defunct—and proper satisfaction,
> But to be free and bounteous to her mind;
> And heaven defend your good souls that you think
> I will your serious and great business scant
> When she is with me.   (1.3.262–68)

Because of the crux in lines 263–64 the speech is not entirely clear, but there is no warrant, I think, for seeing a pathological sexual defensiveness in it. Desdemona's request, in wartime, is unusual, and Othello wants her to be with him at the same time he wishes to assure the senators that they can rely on him to fulfill his office. So he points out, what we already have reason to accept, that he is a mature and moderate man, that he is not driven by appetite and heat, and that he knows how to value Desdemona for her companionship and spirit. At the same time, whatever the syntax, "the young affects" are those that are defunct, and there is no suggestion in the remainder of the speech that he does not expect or wish to consummate his marriage. His emphasis, in this highly public statement, is on the propriety of his behavior as a general as well as an older man. Elizabethans would have had far more sympathy than we do with both concerns: they took the decorum of public life more seriously, and they did not idolize youth or its appetites. Later, on the first night in Cyprus, with the threat of war over, Othello explicitly invites his wife to bed in language that blends scriptural and physical allusiveness:

> Come, my dear love,
> The purchase made, the fruits are to ensue.
> The profit's yet to come 'tween me and you.   (2.3.8–10)

There is no question, except for those critics who would prefer the play to be hiding a novel within it, that the marriage is consummated. Nor is there any suggestion in the behavior of the two the morning after that the consummation has not been pleasurable.

The evocation of January and May, moreover, has a further purpose than simple inversion, for Shakespeare uses Othello's age, as he does his blackness, to dramatize the elemental composition of his marriage. As we have seen, the emphasis in the depiction of Othello's blackness is strongly, though by no means exclusively, religious; the deeper connotations of his age are developed in more psychological terms. January figures were commonly depicted in the second childhood of senility. Shakespeare, in his genius, appropriates the convention to give Othello much of the primal character of a child. A professional soldier, a stranger to Venetian culture and sophistication, and coming to marriage late in life, he seems innocent as well as vulnerable and, without in the least depriving him of his actual manhood, Shakespeare endows him with many of the emotional responses and much of the peculiar vision of a very young boy. What Northrop Frye has described as the "curious quality in Othello's imagination that can only be called cosmological," and what G. Wilson

Knight has discriminated in a different way as "the *Othello* music" are both functions of that vision.[17] They both spring from the primal world of a child's feelings and fantasies, and Othello's habitation in that world at once defines the exotic, "fairy-tale" inflection of his character[18] and is a potent source of his heroic energy throughout the play.[19] In the early acts the accent is on a child's primitive capacity for wonder and worship, and it is demonstrated in Othello's "rude" speech as well as in the life-history he runs through for Brabantio:

> even from my boyish days
> To th' very moment that he bade me tell it,
> Wherein I spake of most disastrous chances,
> Of moving accidents by food and field,
> Of hairbreadth scapes i'th' imminent deadly breach,
> Of being taken by the insolent foe
> And sold to slavery, of my redemption thence,
> And portance in my traveller's history,
> Wherein of antres vast and deserts idle,
> Rough quarries, rock, and hills whose heads touch heaven,
> It was my hint to speak. Such was the process,
> And of the cannibals that each other eat,
> The Anthropophagi, and men whose heads
> Do grow beneath their shoulders.   (1.3.131–44)

Othello's capacity to generate wonder is ultimately an expression of his capacity to feel it, and it is his own childlike wonder and reverence that makes his love for Desdemona in the early acts so remarkable. A human being's first erotic as well as life-giving relationship is with his mother, toward whom he develops intense feelings of affection and desire. Freud argued that a child initially experiences his mother and her nourishment as a virtual extension of himself: "We say that a human being has originally two sexual objects—himself and the woman who nurses him—and in doing so we are postulating a primary narcissism in everyone." In infancy both the mother and the child experience a sense of symbiotic union, and that sense continues in a child's early development, as his "possession" of his mother and her love become an objectification of his most idealized vision of himself. Eventually, of course, with his father both an obstacle and a support, a boy surrenders much of his narcissism and learns to transfer his erotic feelings from himself and his mother to other women, but a man's image of his mother is never lost and, in his deepest and most complete sexual relationships, his early sense of union with his mother, "the primal condition in which object-libido and ego-libido cannot be distinguished," remains the model of sexual ecstasy and the source of his most passionate as well as exalted romantic feelings. Freud himself concluded that no marriage is secure "until the wife has succeeded in making her husband her child as well and in acting as a mother to him." [19]

Desdemona from first to last expresses these primal ideals in her love for Othello, a love that like a mother's is literally unconditional, though at the same time it is freely sexual, and at the beginning Othello responds to it with corresponding primal force. He invests his whole being in his love for her, and in the early acts he always speaks of and to her with that sense of symbiotic exaltation that is the remembrance of childhood, a sense that reaches its apogee in Cyprus, when they are reunited after their journey over "the enchafèd flood":

> *Enter Othello and Attendants.*
> *Othello*   (to Desdemona)
>   O my fair warrior!
> *Desdemona*   My dear Othello.
> *Othello*   It gives me wonder great as my content
>   To see you here before me. O my soul's joy,
>   If after every tempest come such calms,
>   May the winds blow till they have wakened death,
>   And let the labouring barque climb hills of seas
>   Olympus-high, and duck again as low
>   As hell's from heaven. If it were now to die
>   'Twere now to be most happy, for I fear
>   My soul hath her content so absolute

That not another comfort like to this
Succeeds in unknown fate.
Desdemona   The heavens forbid
But that our loves and comforts should increase
Even as our days do grow.
Othello   Amen to that, sweet powers!
I cannot speak enough of this content.
It stops me here, it is too much of joy.
And this, *(they kiss)* and this, the greatest discords be
That e'er our hearts shall make.   (2.1.183–199)

Freud observes, in discussing the love for which a man leaves father and mother to cleave to his wife, that the greatest intensity of sensual passion in men brings with it an overestimation of the object. He argues that "this sexual overvaluation is the origin of the peculiar state of being in love," and that its deepest impulse is to recapture the early feelings of childhood: "To be their own ideal once more, in regard to sexual no less than other trends, as they were in childhood—this is what people strive to attain as their happiness."[20] Freud's discussion of narcissism suggests perhaps an underlying psychological reason for the prominence of images of mirrors in medieval and Renaissance erotic literature.[21] It is also closely analogous to the biblical theme of the regaining of Eden, an eternal "world of original identity," and in art, as Northrop Frye points out, the theme frequently takes the form of a "return . . . not to childhood but to a state of innocence symbolized by childhood." Frye remarks also that in romance literature "the traditional symbolic basis of the sexual quest, which goes back to the Song of Songs in the Bible, is the identification of the mistress' body with the paradisal garden."[22]

The association of Desdemona with such symbolism is particularly strong in *Othello* (and accounts in part for Shakespeare's great insistence on her innocence), and Othello's reunion with her on Cyprus, the most ecstatic moment of the play, draws deeply on the primal psychological and religious sources of all erotic yearning. The movement of desire and feeling in Othello expresses precisely the state of being in love Freud describes, and it suggests as well the striving for the infinite that Frye identifies with the heroic energy of tragedy.[23] The whole of the scene is infused with visual and verbal hyperboles of erotic exaltation. G. Wilson Knight writes that in this scene Othello is "essential man," Desdemona "essential woman," and that "here especially Othello appears a prince of heroes, Desdemona is lit by a divine feminine radiance: both are transfigured."[24] I think that Knight does not exaggerate. The scene is incandescent, and any interpretation that ignores its primal beauty and power is substituting a different play for the one Shakespeare wrote.

At the same time, of course, Othello's association of his joy with dying offers a premonition of the tragedy that is to follow, for the absoluteness of his love brings with it the intimation of death that is incipient within symbiotic union. But Othello is in this respect typical of Shakespeare's tragic heroes, not pathologically different from them. "Because the heroic is above the normal limits of experience," as Frye observes, it is always clear that its "infinite" energies are "imprisoned in the finite" and "driving towards death."[25] The distinction of *Othello* is that this essential tragic action is imagined in erotic terms. In Freud's thought, the state of primary narcissism is itself the crossroads of *eros* and *thanatos*, of the life and death drives in human development. It provides the original model of the self's movement toward others, but it is also the model of the condition in which the self destructively seeks to incorporate others and in which the dissolution of the boundary between the self and others represents the movement toward the "absolute content" of death itself.[26] Macbeth, as we shall see, represents this destructive movement quite directly. Othello clearly verges upon it when he speaks of wakening death and says, "If it were now to die, / 'Twere now to be most happy." But Othello's invocation of the dark side of primary narcissism, unlike Macbeth's, is a function of love and is never separable from it. As Othello speaks, with Iago—who embodies that darkness—as witness, we recognize his profound and inescapable vulnerability, and we may also find tremors of ambivalence and anxiety in what he says,[27] but given that very vulnerability his anxiety is justified and acts in this scene as a measure of the extraordinary heroism of his hope and of his love. Iago, unlike his modern critical affiliates, does not mistake the beauty of what he sees:

> O, you are well tuned now,
> But I'll set down the pegs that make this music,
> As honest as I am.
>
> (2.1.200–202)

Iago, of course, succeeds in his malevolent quest. He does so because in a tragic universe he is an inescapable part of a love like Othello's, because "he represents," as F. R. Leavis says, "something that is in Othello—in Othello the husband of Desdemona: the essential traitor is within the gates." Leavis's conclusion that Othello's love is therefore a pretense from the start and that the play boils down to a study of "an obtuse and brutal egotism" seems to me not to follow and indeed to misconstrue the nature both of egotism and tragedy, but I think his initial perception is undeniable.[28] Shakespeare suggests in the simplest mechanics of the opening dialogue of the temptation scene, through Iago's insistent echoing of Othello's own words, that the process we are to witness is fundamentally an internal one:

Iago   My noble lord.
Othello   What dost thou say, Iago?
Iago   Did Michael Cassio, when you wooed my lady,
      Know of your love?
Othello   He did, from first to last. Why dost thou ask?
Iago   But for a satisfaction of my thought,
      No further harm.
Othello   Why of thy thought, Iago?
Iago   I did not think he had been acquainted with her.
Othello   O yes, and went between us very oft.
Iago   Indeed?
Othello   Indeed? Ay, indeed. Discern'st thou aught in that?
      Is he not honest?
Iago   Honest, my lord?
Othello   Honest? Ay, honest.
Iago   My lord, for aught I know.

Othello   What dost thou think?
Iago   Think, my lord?
Othello   "Think, my lord?" By heaven, thou echo'st me
   As if there were some monster in thy thought
   Too hideous to be shown!   (3.3.94–112)

Iago's words, in this exchange, literally emanate from Othello. Iago is certainly the aggressor, but Othello is clearly ready to respond, and it is he who actively makes the association between the words Iago repeats and the threatening thought behind them. It is he who introduces the pregnant words *honest* and *think*, and it is he, as well as Iago, who creates the monstrous collocation between the two. The dialogue thus schematically represents what the remainder of the temptation scene demonstrates, that Iago echoes something within Othello, that he is a projection of a part of Othello's own psyche.

Iago's psychomachic role would have been unmistakable to Elizabethans. Bernard Spivack has argued that most of Iago's salient stage characteristics, like Richard III's, are drawn from the figure of the Vice.[29] His stage-managing, his artistry in evil that Bradley was the first to emphasize, his aggression through deceit, his corruption of the word, his persistent asides, his intimate relationship with the audience, his vaudevillian gusto, and above all his apparent motivelessness except for the instinct to destroy: all these features of Iago were conventional attributes of the Vice. More recent, and persuasive, scholarship has suggested, as Othello does when he looks down at Iago's feet at the end of the play, that he is more akin to the devil, and there is considerable evidence that devils and Vices had similar stage characteristics.[30] The distinction is not a small one, because as a Vice, Iago would be an allegorical expression purely of Othello's own inner disposition to viciousness, whereas as the devil, he dramatizes a temptation to evil that exists both without and within Othello. The difference is most important to our response to the play and we shall return to it, but for the moment we should recognize that in either case Iago represents as deep a wellspring in Othello's soul as Desdemona does and carries as great a religious and psychological resonance.

The theological dynamics of Iago's usurpation of Desdemona's place in Othello's being is quite explicit, and its essential locus is once again Othello's (and Desdemona's) color. Iago repeatedly associates his diabolic auspices with the capacity to invert darkness and light:

> Hell and night
> Must bring this monstrous birth to the world's light.
> (1.3.395–96)

> Divinity of hell:
> When devils will the blackest sins put on,
> They do suggest at first with heavenly shows,
> As I do now.
> (2.3.341–44)

It is at the end of the latter speech that he promises to turn Desdemona's "virtue into pitch," and he fulfills that promise, ultimately, because he succeeds in making Othello believe only in the letter of his own blackness. When Brabantio first taunts Othello to look to Desdemona if he has "eyes to see," Othello answers, as we have seen, with a testimony of faith that is subsumed by Desdemona's vision of him, "I saw Othello's visage in his mind." Midway in the temptation scene, however, once Iago's thoughts, and his own, have begun to take effect, he tells Iago:

> Nor from mine own weak merits will I draw
> The smallest fear or doubt of her revolt,
> For she had eyes and chose me. No, Iago,
> I'll see before I doubt; when I doubt, prove;
> And, on the proof, there is no more but this:
> Away at once with love or jealousy.
> (3.3.191–96)

This speech is the immediate prelude to his fall, as well as the predication of it, for once he accepts the epistemology of "normal" Venetian eyesight, he is doomed. After reminding him that Desdemona, "so young could give out such a seeming, / To seel her father's eyes up close as oak (3.3.213–14), Iago can easily persuade him that there must be something monstrous in Desdemona's love for him, and it is an inevitable step to the conclusion that

> My name, that was as fresh
> As Dian's visage, is now begrimed and black
> As mine own face. (3.3.391–93)

It is no exaggeration to suggest, given the pervasive spiritual connotations of blackness in the play, that at this point Othello has lost his faith and is in a state of despair. The godlike presumption that masks his subsequent vengeance—"This sorrow's heavenly, / It strikes where it doth love" (5.2.21–22)—only confirms that inner state, as does his increasing incapacity to accept or believe in Desdemona's love. His eventual destruction of her is itself an irremissable, suicidal act. He has loved her as his own flesh, and when he destroys her, he destroys the basis of his own existence. And he knows it:

> My wife, my wife! What wife? I ha' no wife.
> O, insupportable, O heavy hour!
> Methinks it should be now a huge eclipse
> Of sun and moon, and that th'affrighted globe
> Should yawn at alteration. (5.2.106–10)

The psychoanalytic ramifications of Iago's aggression against Othello, which is to say, Othello's aggression against himself, have a comparable effect. Iago is Desdemona's sexual as well as spiritual antagonist. Where she luminously represents a union of affection and desire, Iago wishes to reduce love to "merely a lust of the blood and a permission of the will" (1.3.334–35). He repeatedly assures Roderigo that the love of Desdemona and Othello cannot last, that by its very nature it must fail:

> The food that to him now is as luscious as locusts shall
> be to him shortly as bitter as coloquintida. She must
> change for youth. When she is sated with his body, she
> will find the error of her choice. (1.3.347–51)

Mark me with what violence she first loved the Moor,
but for bragging and telling her fantastical lies. To love
him still for prating?—let not thy discreet heart think it.
Her eye must be fed, and what delight shall she have to
look on the devil? When the blood is made dull with the
act of sport, there should be again to inflame it, and to
give satiety a fresh appetite, loveliness in favour, sympathy in years, manners, and beauties, all which the Moor
is defective in. Now, for want of these required conve-
niences, her delicate tenderness will find itself abused,
begin to heave the gorge, disrelish and abhor the Moor.
Very nature will instruct her in it and compel her to
some second choice.   (2.1.223–35)

Considering the number of critics who, like Auden, end up
agreeing with Iago's assumptions, it should be noted that Iago is
speaking to Roderigo, the simplest of gulls (and even he objects),
and speaking disingenuously. As Iago's soliloquies show, his deepest animus against Othello and Desdemona stems precisely from
his belief that their "free and open nature" makes them capable
of proving him wrong. The basic motive of his malignancy, like
Satan's, is envy.

Iago nevertheless prevails with Othello, as I have already suggested, because Othello eventually internalizes Iago's maleficent
sexual vision and sees himself with Iago's eyes, rather than Desdemona's; and again the nexus of his vulnerability, as of his romantic disposition, is his age and color. At a critical turn in the
argument of the temptation scene, Othello wonders that "nature" should be "erring from itself" in Desdemona (3.3.232). It
is a line that could be construed and meant as a protest against
Iago's insinuations, but Iago quickly transforms it into a deeply
subversive sexual indictment:

Ay, there's the point: as, to be bold with you,
Not to affect many proposèd matches
Of her own clime, complexion, and degree,
Whereto we see in all things nature tends.

Foh, one may smell in such a will most rank,
Foul disproportions, thoughts unnatural!　　　(3.3.233–38)

Shortly afterwards, Othello adopts those thoughts as his own, and explicitly associates them with his color and his age:

> Haply for I am black
> And have not those soft parts of conversation
> That chamberers have; or for I am declined
> Into the vale of years—yet that's not much—
> She's gone. I am abused, and my relief
> Must be to loathe her. O curse of marriage,
> That we can call these delicate creatures ours
> And not their appetites!　　　(3.3.267–74)

This is the crux of Othello's fall, and his union with Iago's world of blood lust follows immediately. He believes that Desdemona cannot be true because he becomes convinced that he himself is unlovable and, believing that, he also becomes convinced that Desdemona's manifest attraction to him is itself perverse, a "proof" of her corruption. Just before he strangles her, he and she have the following extremely painful dialogue:

Othello　Think on thy sins.
Desdemona　They are loves I bear to you.
Othello　Ay, and for that thou diest.
Desdemona　That death's unnatural that kills for loving.
　　　　　　　(5.2.42–45)

I am not altogether sure what these lines mean. Desdemona may be referring to the sin of disobeying her father. Othello may be condemning Desdemona for her very desire for him, or he may be projecting upon her his incapacity to accept his own desires, probably both. And hovering over the lines may be the sense of guilt of the original sin, which was at once physical and spiritual. But whatever their precise meaning, the lines convey the ultimate horror of the play, which is Othello's destructive transmutation of the precept upon which his, or any, marriage is founded: "So men are bound to love their wives as their own bodies. He that loveth his own wife, loveth himself." The tragedy of Othello is that finally he fails to love his own body, to love himself, and it is this despairing self-hatred that spawns the suicidal destructiveness of his jealousy. In a Renaissance manual of psychology, Pierre Charron says of jealousy "that the only meane to avoid it, is for a man to make himselfe worthie of that he desireth, for jealousie is nothing else but a distrust of our selves, and a testimonie of our little desert." [31]

The awesome energy of Othello's jealousy, its primitive and superstitious murderousness, is a function of the same primal forces that animated his earlier exaltation and love. As a child matures, he must inevitably be separated from his mother, he must confront the reality first that he cannot incorporate her, that she is not a part of him, and then that she has a sexual love for his father from which he is obviously and necessarily excluded. In the Freudian cosmology this conflict is inescapable, and the child, before he experiences his inevitable oedipal defeat and learns to reconstitute himself, experiences profound feelings of betrayal and rivalry and threats of the loss of identity and of nurture. It is this constellation of feelings that is the primal source of sexual jealousy and that is tapped directly in the second half of *Othello*:

> But, alas, to make me
> A fixèd figure for the time of scorn
> To point his slow and unmoving finger at—
> Yet could I bear that too, well, very well.
> But there where I have garnered up my heart,
> Where either I must live or bear no life,
> The fountain from the which my current runs
> Or else dries up—to be discarded thence,
> Or keep it as a cistern for foul toads
> To knot and gender in! Turn thy complexion there,
> Patience, thou young and rose-lipped cherubin,
> Ay, here look grim as hell. (4.2.55–66)

This is not a pleasant passage to contemplate, but it is very important to an understanding of the play, for its conflation of images of the breast and of the womb expresses a precise etiology of Othello's jealous anguish.

The passage also suggests a literalization of the Friar's observation in *Romeo and Juliet* that "The earth, that's nature's mother, is her tomb. / What is her burying grave, that is her womb" (2.2.9–10) and in such terms it intimates the residue in Othello of the infantile fear of being enveloped and devoured.[32] But it is important to remember that in these same terms Othello's anguish expresses the larger experience of mortality that confronts all of Shakespeare's titanic heroes. For his commitment to a love that is so absolutely rooted in, and dependent upon, symbiotic union, translates him to a realm in which, as we have noted, the drives of life and death are themselves indistinguishable.

The symbiotic character of Othello's union with Desdemona is also suggested in Shakespeare's treatment of the handkerchief, the accidental hinge of the plot whose "triviality" has so bedeviled the play's critics from Rymer onwards. "That handkerchief," Othello first explains,

> Did an Egyptian to my mother give.
> She was a charmer, and could almost read
> The thoughts of people. She told her, while she kept it
> 'Twould make her amiable, and subdue my father
> Entirely to her love; but if she lost it,
> Or made a gift of it, my father's eye
> Should hold her loathèd, and his spirits should hunt
> After new fancies.   (3.4.55–63)

The superstitious cast of this speech is a regression not merely to Othello's literally primitive past, but to the primitive world of a child's merger with his mother, and there is already implicit in what Othello says the sense of his own primal betrayal. It is not then essentially an accident that the handkerchief should become coextensive in his mind with his jealous fantasy of Desdemona's betrayal of him and with his thoughts of revenge: "Lie with her. Lie on her? We say 'lie on her' when they belie her. Lie with her? 'Swounds, that's fulsome! Handkerchief—confessions—handkerchief. To confess and be hanged for his labour. First, to be hanged and then to confess! I tremble at it. Nature would not invest herself in such shadowing passion without some instruction. It is not words that shakes me thus. Pish! Noses, ears, and lips! Is't possible? Confess? Handkerchief? O devil! *He falls down in a trance*" (4.1.34–42). What has clearly become insupportable for Othello in this scene is the fulsomeness of his own sexual instincts,[33] but the dislocated syntax and deep conflations of actions and of parts of the body in this passage also suggests the primitive realm of symbiosis in its most threatening aspect, its sensation of the loss of integrity and of life itself.

In a broad sense, Othello's behavior in the second half of the play is a dramatization of guilt. In Christian terms the temptation scene recollects the Fall of Man, which brought death into the world and which Augustine interpreted as an allegorical representation of an essentially psychomachic process, the disorder of the soul by which reason becomes subjected to passion, and particularly the self-destroying as well as self-exalting passion of pride. In analogous psychoanalytic terms, the guilt is the aggression of the unconscious, again an internal process, in which Iago represents one part of Othello and Desdemona another and in which his destruction of Desdemona represents a direct function of his exaltation of her. I do not think it follows, however, as many theological and psychological critics seem to believe, that the play is therefore throughout or essentially a pathological study either of an idolator or a narcissist, however many attributes of both Othello may in fact demonstrate. It seems to me, on the contrary, for a number of reasons, that such approaches profoundly misconstrue, where they do not utterly ignore, the play's actual experience.

To begin with, and one cannot overemphasize the point, Desdemona is as much a part of Othello's soul, whether spiritually or psychically conceived, as Iago. In actual life so absolutely loving and forgiving a wife is no doubt a human impossibility, a fantasy. But in the play she is not a fantasy, or rather she is a fantasy made flesh: the life, not just the imago, of that union of tenderness and desire, that unconditional love, toward which all men aspire. Othello marries her, and the whole first half of the play celebrates his incandescent erotic feelings for her; in the second half his torment and decomposition can be measured, as they always are in his own consciousness, by his loss of her. Even in the midst of his savagery his soul remains vivified by her loveliness: "O, the world hath not a sweeter creature! . . . But yet the pity of it, Iago. O, Iago, the pity of it, Iago!" (4.1.189–90, 191–92). It is deeply fitting in his final speech, and cheering to us if not to him, that his dying recognition that she was true should enable him genuinely to recover a sense of his former being, just as his delusion that she was faithless caused him to lose it.[34]

Correspondingly, Iago does not constitute the whole of Othello's spiritual state or of his unconscious. He is not simply a projection of Othello's own disposition to vice, though of course he plays upon it. He is not a Vice but, as he himself repeatedly announces and everyone else in the play eventually realizes, a "hellish villain" (5.2.378). He is the eternal tempter who succeeds because he attacks in Othello not just his frailty but the frailty of all men. W. H. Auden suggests, astutely, that Iago "treats Othello as an analyst treats a patient except that, of course, his intention is to kill not to cure." Auden goes on to observe that everything Iago says "is designed to bring to Othello's consciousness what he has already guessed is there";[35] but a further and crucial point should be made, which is that what is "there" exists as part of the unconscious life of all men. It is not peculiar to Othello, though it is tragically heightened in him. The issue is not an abstract one in *Othello*, because within the world that Shakespeare creates in the play honest Iago is a spokesman for what everyone else, save Desdemona, feels or believes or represents. Othello's guilt, in fact, pervades his society, and Iago has only to return to him the image of himself that he can see reflected, not in fantasy but in reality, in the world about him. Brabantio, who was formerly his friend, who "loved" and "oft invited" him to his house, vilifies him and believes that Desdemona is bewitched and that the marriage is obscene; and the opening scene of the play implicates us as well as Venetian soci-

ety in this deep racial prejudice. Cassio idolizes Desdemona and
at the same time is capable of a sexual relationship only with a
whore of whom he is essentially contemptuous. And in a proleptic version of Othello's fall, he gets drunk and violent on Othello's wedding night. The only other marriage in the play is Iago's
and Emilia's, and although Emilia's portrayal is very complex, it is
nevertheless obvious that Iago has little affection for her and
that at least the premises of her own worldly realism are not far
from his. Only at the end, in a response to Desdemona's fidelity
that neither she nor certainly Iago would ever have anticipated,
does she move into another realm of feeling and value, and even
then she finds Desdemona's marriage incomprehensible, if not
repellent: "She was too fond of her most filthy bargain"
(5.2.164). It is no wonder that Othello, literally an alien by his
profession, his background, his color, and his age, should in such
a world find it tragically impossible to hold to the scriptural belief, which is also Desdemona's, that he is "black, but beautiful."
Freud remarked in *Civilization and Its Discontents* that "in an individual neurosis we take as our starting-point the contrast that
distinguishes the patient from his environment, which is assumed to be 'normal.' "[36] No such assumption can be made about
the environment of *Othello* either in Venice or Cyprus. It is not
normal, it is itself guilt-ridden, and Othello is at once its victim
and its heroic sacrifice.

In a tragic universe, it is worth stressing, guilt, like death, is
inescapable, and the hero commands our minds and hearts not
because he is a good or a bad man, or because he is saved or
damned, but because he most deeply incarnates and experiences
the inexorable tragic conditions that we recognize in our own
existence. In *Othello* those conditions are primarily and explicitly
sexual, whether they are understood in religious or psychological
terms, and from an Elizabethan or modern perspective. Freud's
own view, expressed consistently in his writing, is that the oedipal drama which forms the basis of human development is fundamentally tragic, and in the essay from which I quoted at the
start of this discussion, "The Most Prevalent Form of Degradation in Erotic Life," he argues that the dissociation of affection
and sensuality that characterizes cases of actual psychical impo-

tence is in the last analysis a condition of all human beings; that the two currents of erotic feeling, "the same two that are personified in art as heavenly and earthly (or animal) love," are rarely completely fused in civilized man. He remarks: "It has an ugly sound and a paradoxical as well, but nevertheless it must be said that whoever is to be really free and happy in love must have overcome his deference for women and come to terms with the idea of incest with mother or sister. Anyone who in the face of this test subjects himself to serious self-examination will indubitably find that at the bottom of his heart he too regards the sexual act as something degrading, which soils and contaminates not only the body." Freud concludes that "however strange it may sound, I think the possibility must be considered that something in the nature of the sexual instinct itself is unfavorable to the achievement of complete gratification."[37] The whole of this essay is the nucleus of Freud's later, more celebrated, discussion of aggression and guilt in *Civilization and Its Discontents*.

Freud, of course, did not originate these ideas. Similar concepts are inherent and often developed in a considerable body of medieval and Renaissance literature combining erotic and theological themes, and in his own time Shakespeare would have found them stated with Freudian explicitness in Montaigne's "Upon Some Verses of *Virgil*," the essay from which he almost certainly drew directly in *All's Well that Ends Well*. Since Montaigne actually tended himself to degrade women, he demonstrates as well as parallels Freud's thought. His essay deals with sexuality, and a large part of it constitutes an argument against the possibility of uniting the affection that belongs to marriage and the *"insatiate thirst of enjoying a greedily desired subject"* that belongs to sensual love: *"Love disdaineth a man should hold of other then himselfe,* and dealeth but faintly with acquaintances begun and entertained under another title; as mariage is. . . . Nor is it other then a kinde of incest, in this reverent alliance and sacred bond, to employ the efforts and extravagant humor of an amorous licentiousnes. . . . Wedlocke hath for his share honour, justice, profit and constancie: a plaine, but more generall delight. Love melts in onely pleasure." Like Freud, Montaigne finds something paradoxically degrading about the very "acte of generation":

In al other things you may observe decorum and main-
taine some decency: all other operations admit some
rules of honesty: this cannot onely be imagined, but vicious or ridiculous. . . . Surely it is an argument not onely
of our originall corruption, but a badge of our vanity
and deformity. On the one side nature urgeth us unto
it: having thereunto combined, yea fastned, the most
noble, the most profitable, and the most sensually-
pleasing, of all her functions: and on the other suffereth
us to accuse, to condemne and to shunne it, as insolent,
as dishonest, and as lewder to blush at it, and allow, yea
and to commend abstinence. *Are not we most brutish, to
terme that worke beastly which begets, and which maketh us?*

Montaigne, like Freud, observes the ultimate incapacity of erotic
instincts to be fully satisfied or harmonized: "But withall *it is
against the nature of love, not to be violent, and against the condition of
violence, to be constant. . . . It is not a passion meerely corporeall. If
no end be found in coveteousnesse, nor limit in ambition, assure your selfe
there is nor end nor limit in letchery.* It yet continueth after saciety:
nor can any man prescribe it or end or constant satisfaction: it
ever goeth on beyond it's possession, beyond it's bounds." Montaigne says finally of marriage that "it is a match wherto may well
be applied the common saying, *homo homini aut Deus, aut Lupus
. . . Man unto man is either a God or a Wolfe.*" [38]
    It is within this polarized erotic universe that Othello moves,
and he traverses its extremes not only in the larger parabolic
action of the creation and death of his marriage, but in the very
constitution of his being. At the very hinge of the play's action,
just after Desdemona leaves him with her pleas for Cassio, and
the instant before Iago begins his attack, Othello says,

> Excellent wretch! Perdition catch my soul
> But I do love thee, and when I love thee not,
> Chaos is come again.   (3.3.91–93)

These well-known lines spring from the heart of Othello's existence and describe the essence of the paradox that at once ani-

mates and destroys him. They can be construed as ultimately yielding only "an honourable murderer" and an object that "poisons sight" (5.2.300, 374), but like the play itself the lines represent a tragedy not a homily, and the paradoxical essence of the tragedy is that the chaos and death of Othello's love is at one with its deepest life. At the end, in his last words, I think Othello speaks the truth, both of his experience and of our response to it, when he says that he is "one that loved not wisely but too well" (5.2.353). The play has deep affiliations with romance. It is a full and moving tragic anatomy of love, not a clinical diagnosis or demonstration, and Othello is its hero not because he achieves triumph or suffers defeat, though he does both, nor because he learns or does not learn a theological or psychological lesson, but because he is indeed, as Cassio says, "great of heart," and because he enacts for us, with beautiful and terrifying nakedness, the primitive energies that are the substance of our own erotic lives.

CHAPTER IV

MACBETH

MACBETH IS THE MOST SELF-CENTERED of Shakespeare's tragic heroes and, not coincidentally, the one with the least amplitude of spirit. All of Shakespeare's great tragic figures are isolated in a universe essentially of their own imagination and thought, but in none of them is such isolation so inordinate and destructive an expression of egoism as it is in Macbeth.[1] Macbeth relentlessly pursues what he thinks of as his "own good" (3.4.134), but the more he does so, the more diminished he becomes. The charge that "he is old Iron Pants in the field" but that "at home" Lady Macbeth "has to wear the pants" is not entirely outrageous: his frequent domination by his wife is symptomatic.[2] He provokes desires in himself that he is increasingly incapable of satisfying, and he seems from the first "cabined, cribbed, confined, bound in / To saucy doubts and fears" (3.4.23–24). These characteristics make Macbeth a peculiarly difficult hero to sympathize with, let alone admire, but they are central to his tragedy, and they should be dealt with in their own terms, not sentimentalized, ignored, or—as is the recent fashion—turned on their heads.

In *The City of God* St. Augustine calls the pride from which man's and Satan's rebellion resulted "a perverse desire of height," and his discussion both of the nature of this desire and of its consequences is extremely germane to an understanding of Macbeth's characterization. "What is pride," Augustine writes, "but a perverse desire of height, in forsaking Him to whom the soul ought solely to cleave, as the beginning thereof, to make itself seem its own beginning. This is when it likes itself too well, or when it so loves itself that it will abandon that unchangeable Good which ought to be more delightful to it than itself." Since man was created of nothing, Augustine continues, he was "lessened in excellence" at the Fall: by "leaving Him to adhere to and delight in himself, he grew not to be nothing, but towards nothing." The devil said to Adam and Eve, " 'Ye shall be as gods': which they might sooner have been by obedience and coherence with their Creator than by proud opinion that they were their own beginners; for the created gods are not gods of themselves but by participation of the God that made them; but man desiring more became less, and choosing to be sufficient in himself fell from that all-sufficient God." The just reward, Augustine concludes, that Adam and Eve received for "desiring more" was the perpetuation of the paradox of that desire: "What is man's misery other than his own disobedience to himself: that seeing he would not what he might, now he cannot what he would? For although in paradise all was not in his power during his obedience, yet then he desired nothing but what was in his power, and so did what he would. But now, as the scripture says and we see by experience, 'man is like to vanity.' For who can recount his innumerable desires of impossibilities?" [3]

An interest in the futility and suffering that Augustine associates with self-love can be seen early in Shakespeare's career in *The Rape of Lucrece*, a work that not only anticipates *Macbeth* but is also, together with *Richard III*, its most deeply suggestive source.[4] Though the poem's ostensible subject is rape, the lust it portrays is primarily an expression of pride and ambition. Tarquin's resolve to possess Lucrece is repeatedly and explicitly associated with envy, usurpation, and competition at the same time that it is treated as a violent instance of man's general perversity in "desiring more." The prose argument and early lines of the poem make clear that Tarquin—whose father, "for his excessive pride," was "surnamed Superbus" (Argument)—is provoked to desire Lucrece in the first place because of his "envy" of her husband Collatine's possessing "so rich a thing" (39), and this underlying motive is given acute emphasis just before the rape, as Tarquin views Lucrece's sleeping figure:

> Her breasts like ivory globes circled with blue,
> A pair of maiden worlds unconquerèd,
> Save of their lord, no bearing yoke they knew,
> And him by oath they truly honourèd.
> These worlds in Tarquin new ambition bred,
>> Who like a foul usurper went about
>> From this fair throne to heave the owner out. (407–13)

Shakespeare suggests the Augustinian understanding of Tarquin's "ambition" throughout *The Rape of Lucrece*. "Nothing in him seemed inordinate," Shakespeare remarks at the start of the poem:

> Save sometime too much wonder of his eye,
> Which having all, all could not satisfy,
>> But poorly rich so wanteth in his store
>> That, cloyed with much, he pineth still for more.
>>> (94–96)

The self-destructive consequences of such desire are homiletically elaborated as Tarquin lies in his own bed "revolving / The sundry dangers of his will's obtaining":

> Those that much covet are with gain so fond
> That what they have not, that which they possess,
> They scatter and unloose it from their bond,
> And so by hoping more they have but less,
> Or, gaining more, the profit of excess
>> Is but to surfeit and such griefs sustain
>> That they prove bankrupt in this poor-rich
>> gain. . . .

> So that, in vent'ring ill, we leave to be
> The things we are for that which we expect,
> And this ambitious foul infirmity

In having much, torments us with defect
Of that we have; so then we do neglect
　　The thing we have, and all for want of wit
　　Make something nothing by augmenting it.

Such hazard now must doting Tarquin make,
Pawning his honor to obtain his lust,
And for himself himself he must forsake.

(127–28, 134–40, 148–57)

The same paradoxes are emphasized during as well as after the rape. Tarquin's appetite, repeatedly referred to as the "pride" of his flesh (438, 705, 712), is compared with "drunken desire," that "must vomit his receipt / Ere he can see his own abomination" (703–4), and with "vulture folly / A swallowing gulf that even in plenty wanteth" (557); and he is ultimately dismissed from the poem as "A captive victor that hath lost in gain" (730).[5]

There are numerous precise parallels between *The Rape of Lucrece* and *Macbeth*. The line "And for himself himself he must forsake," for example, looks forward suggestively both to Macbeth's fear of knowing himself (2.2.71) and to his fear that his "single state of man" is literally disintegrating, that parts of his body are separating from him; and Shakespeare describes Tarquin's internal debate before the rape in terms that anticipate the external debate between Macbeth and Lady Macbeth before the murder of Duncan: "Thus graceless holds he disputation / 'Tween frozen conscience and hot-burning will" (246–47). These lines lend support to Freud's suggestion that Macbeth and Lady Macbeth "complete" each other as characters, that Shakespeare conceived of them as "disunited parts of a single psychical individuality."[6]

All of the antinomies of *The Rape of Lucrece* look forward to *Macbeth*, however, and, as in the play, they are not simply the occasion for moral commentary. They represent the texture of Tarquin's thought. The entire first half of *The Rape of Lucrece* depicts a psychomachia in Tarquin's "inward mind" (185) that is subsumed by paradoxes of self-love. "Madly tossed between desire and dread" (171), Tarquin is continuously shown in self-conscious and self-consuming debates between his "guilt" and his "affection." Though much more richly developed, essentially the same kinds of divisions and debates compose the mental life of Macbeth. Like Tarquin a tormented and spectral figure, literally "a foul usurper," both driven and crippled by "Drunken desire," Macbeth moves toward regicide as Tarquin moves toward rape, similarly torn between desire and dread, in "the dead of night," as *The Rape of Lucrece* states, when "Pure thoughts are dead and still, / While lust and murder wake to stain and kill" (162, 167–68). Just before Duncan's murder, Macbeth explicitly compares himself to Tarquin:

> Now o'er the one half-world
> Nature seems dead, and wicked dreams abuse
> The curtained sleep. Witchcraft celebrates
> Pale Hecate's offerings, and withered murder,
> Alarumed by his sentinel the wolf,
> Whose howl's his watch, thus with his stealthy pace,
> With Tarquin's ravishing strides, towards his design
> Moves like a ghost.   (2.1.49–56)

Echoes of Tarquin's rape of Lucrece and of its larger meaning in Shakespeare's imagination also inform the scene, just after the murder, in which the Porter comments on the literal effect of drunkenness upon sexual desire: "Lechery, sir, it provokes and unprovokes: it provokes the desire but it takes away the performance. Therefore much drink may be said to be an equivocator with lechery: it makes him and it mars him; it sets him on and it takes him off; it persuades him and disheartens him, makes him stand to and not stand to; in conclusion, equivocates him in a sleep, and, giving him the lie, leaves him" (2.3.28–35). The relevance of this bawdy speech to the profoundest movements of the play can hardly be exaggerated.[7] The equivocations of "Drunken desire" are related to those of the witches' prophecies and to a whole world in which "from that spring, whence comfort seemed to come / Discomfort swells" (1.2.27–28). Shakespeare directly associates the equivocations the Porter describes with the garments of ambition that clothe Macbeth: "Was the hope drunk,"

Lady Macbeth asks him, "Wherein you dressed yourself?" (1.7.35–36). And the same equivocations are suggested, if not acted out, in the relationship of Macbeth and Lady Macbeth. With taunts that seem also to be yearnings, Lady Macbeth provokes Macbeth to be more of a man by killing Duncan, and she calls him "My husband!" (2.2.13) for the first and only time right after the killing. But the conjunction of "lust and murder" that thus seems to give new life to their marriage at the same time empties it. After Macbeth has attained the crown, Lady Macbeth cries:

> Naught's had, all's spent,
> Where our desire is got without content.
> 'Tis safer to be that which we destroy
> Than by destruction dwell in doubtful joy.   (3.2.6–9)

Macbeth enters at exactly the moment Lady Macbeth says these lines, and she suppresses her thoughts in trying to woo him away from his. But Macbeth is already moving decisively away from her at the same time that he echoes her:

> Better be with the dead,
> Whom we to gain our peace have sent to peace,
> Than on the torture of the mind to lie
> In restless ecstasy.   (3.2.21–24)

The "restless" condition that the Porter describes may be humorous in a drunk, but in sober and sleepless men and women it suggests hell, which is where Shakespeare locates the Porter and the whole action of the play.[8] The only desire Macbeth and Lady Macbeth subsequently have in common, though they cannot share it, is the desire for extinction.

The suffering that Macbeth and Lady Macbeth endure represents a heightened version of the condition that Renaissance moral philosophers argued was inherent in all human passions. For these commentators, as we have seen, as for earlier Christian writers, all of the passions were perturbations of the mind, expressions of the "innumerable desires of impossibilities" that caused the Fall and constituted man's state forever after it. The passions did not exist when man was at rest in paradise, perfectly at one—at "peace," to use Macbeth's term—with himself and his surroundings, when, in Augustine's words, he "desired nothing but what was in his power, and so did what he would," rather than, as now, what "he cannot." For La Primaudaye, writing in the *The French Academie*, the epitome of this general predicament of human desire is ambition. "Ambition never suffreth those that have once received hir as a guest, to enjoy their present estate quietly," he remarks,

> but maketh them always emptie of goods, and full of hope. It causes them to contemne that, which they have gotten by great paines and travel, and which not long before they desired very earnestly, by reason of their new imaginations and conceites of greater matters, which they continually barke forth, but never have their minds satisfied and contented. And the more they growe and increase in power and authoritie, the rather are they induced and caried headlong by their affections to commit all kind of injustice, and flatter themselves in furious and frantike actions, that they may come to the end of their infinite platformes.[9]

The "infinite platformes" of Macbeth comprehend an appalling measure of destructive as well as insatiable aspiration, and beyond his general observations, La Primaudaye has a number of particular reflections on ambition that are exceptionally apposite to *Macbeth*. He observes, citing Plutarch, that "the desire of having more ... bringeth foorth" in ambitious and great lords "oftentimes an unsociable, cruell, and beastly nature," and he adds: "Further, if (as histories teach us) some have been so wretched & miserable, as to give themselves to the Art of Necromancie, and to contract with the devill, that they might come to soveraigne power and authoritie, what other thing, how strange soever it be, will not they undertake that suffer themselves to be wholly carried away with this vice of ambition? It is ambition that setteth the sonne against the father, and imboldeneth him to seek his destruction of whom he holdeth his life."[10] This remarkable passage shows striking analogies with *Macbeth*. Macbeth makes a pact with witches, if not the devil; Scotland, as the Porter and many others make clear, becomes an "expresse similitude of hell" as a result;[11] and the murder of Duncan "is little else than a parricide."[12] It is Lady Macbeth who explicitly says that the King resembled "My father as he slept" (2.2.13), but she speaks for Macbeth's soul as well, and the association of father and king was in any case inescapable in the Renaissance. It animates as well as haunts Macbeth from the first.[13]

What is ultimately most interesting about the motifs of parricide and necromancy in *Macbeth*, however, is not just their presence but their conjunction in Macbeth's mind (the conjunction, as it were, of the aspiring thoughts of both Marlowe's Tamburlaine and Faustus), for Shakespeare suggests that the two are deeply connected if not actually functions of each other. This connection, which La Primaudaye states explicitly, is at the core of Macbeth's characterization. It is directly related to the dynamics of original sin, the desire for omnipotence that Augustine describes, and at the same time it has precise and illuminating analogues in modern psychological thought. Freud is most celebrated for arguing that the fantasy of killing and replacing the father is the fulcrum of human psychological development. Less familiar and certainly less actively appreciated is his contention that oedipal guilt can have such potency in human development because for a small child a murderous thought is indistinguishable from a murderous deed, and he traces this "necromantic" thinking to the period of primary narcissism.

Because the theme of usurpation is so insistent in *Macbeth*, the play's parricidal resonances are not hard to find. The real issue is to understand them in the proportions and with the particular inflections that the play itself gives to them. In the most directly voluptuous of her fantasies, Lady Macbeth tells Macbeth that the "great business" of murdering the King "shall to all our nights and days to come / Give solely sovereign sway and masterdom" (1.5.67, 68–69). The aspiration to be the only one, to have sole sovereignty, sole masterdom and possession, is the aspect of childhood thinking that has the deepest roots in the psyche and not incidentally the clearest analogue to Augustine's theology of the Fall. In a child's imagination the wish to be the one and only is absolute—it is so by definition—and the result is a particularly deep representation of the Augustinian dialectic of more and less. Very young children, in the unlovely exclusiveness of their egoism, always tend to feel that they are impaired by someone else's gain, that loss is self-diminishment. In the *Confessions* Augustine remarks, "My selfe have seene and observed some little child, who could not speake; and yet he was all in an envious kind of wrath, looking pale with a bitter countenance upon his foster-brother [nursing]"; and Augustine asks if it can be "accounted innocency, that an infant cannot endure a companion to feed with him, in a fountaine of milke, which is richly abounding and overflowing; although that companion be wholly destitute, and can take no other food but that?" [14]

Such primitive envy, moreover, is not confined to children. Montaigne remarks on its persistence in adults in a brief and unsettling essay entitled "The Profit of One Man is the Dammage of Another." He observes that "let every man sound his owne conscience, hee shall finde, that our inward desires are for the most part nourished and bred in us by the losse and hurt of others," and he associates this condition with the "generall policie" of "Nature": "for Physitians hold, that *The birth, increase, and augmentation of every thing, is the alteration and corruption of another*." [15] Freud contends, in his own domestication of these natural laws, that in a very young boy's fantasies of competition with his father this "generall policie" can take on a murderous inflection: heaving the owner out, to use the words of *The Rape of Lucrece*, means killing him.

Precisely such an inflection is in fact given to competitive thinking by Duncan at the very outset of *Macbeth*, when he tells Rosse to "pronounce" the "present death" of the Thane of Cawdor, "And with his former title greet Macbeth. . . . What he hath lost, noble Macbeth hath won" (1.2.64, 65, 67). The inverse and murderous relationship between winning and losing that Duncan reveals in these lines suggests the dialectic that both Montaigne and Freud comment upon, and it describes the actual condition of the whole world of *Macbeth* in its early scenes, for the play suggests the anatomy of a parricidal nightmare long before the Macbeths enact one. The witches initiate the absolute opposition between winning and losing at the very beginning of the play—"When the battle's lost and won" (1.1.4)—and their prophecies are often couched in the language of inverse functions and equivocal contest (being greater or lesser, for example, not so happy or much happier), but the rhetoric of their supernatural solicitations, at least at the start, is quite tangibly anchored in the natural world of the play. Rivalry, "self-comparisons" (1.2.55), is war, and competition is blood in the world of rebellious Scotland; men often must walk in "strange" if not "borrowed" robes; and a man's title and place can literally be defined by killing. Macbeth does in fact, not in fantasy, defeat and replace the Thane of Cawdor and, though he is responsible for Cawdor's death, he is not responsible for the rebellious disorder that is its occasion. Duncan is the "Lord's anointed" (2.3.67), and as Macbeth himself painfully testifies, "clear in his great office" (1.7.18), but if he is a good and rightful king, he is not evidently a strong one, and the darkened realm of ambiguous and bloody contest over which he presides at the start of the play is the political equivalent of the parricidal battleground of a young boy's imagination, a world that invites, in Banquo's phrase, "the cursèd thoughts that nature / Gives way to in repose" (2.1.8–9).

The diffusion of such thoughts in the early part of the play suggests not that Shakespeare is apportioning them for praise or blame, still less that he is using them to create a subversive subtext,[16] but rather that he is presenting them as heightened, tragic conditions of the economy of nature that Montaigne discriminates and that Macbeth himself eventually incarnates. The "cursèd thoughts" of which Banquo speaks are, of course, in Macbeth's own mind from the very beginning. Freud suggests that a man sometimes will commit murder in order to rationalize his sense of guilt, that guilt is the cause of the crime rather than its result.[17] There is more than a suggestion of this condition in Macbeth (as opposed to Lady Macbeth, in whom guilt is a distinct aftereffect). There is a strong sense of forbidden and buried thoughts in Macbeth's rapt reaction to his first meeting with the witches, and these thoughts immediately surface in his first soliloquy when he speaks of the "horrid image" that unseats his heart, of the "horrible imaginings" that surpass his present fears, and of his "thought, whose murder yet is but fantastical," which

> Shakes so [his] single state of man that function
> Is smothered in surmise, and nothing is
> But what is not.   (1.3.134, 137, 138–41)

But the lines that give the sharpest expression to the parricidal thoughts that both surround him and lie within him occur when Duncan proclaims Malcolm Prince of Cumberland and heir to the throne. Macbeth says in an aside:

> The Prince of Cumberland—that is a step
> On which I must fall down or else o'erleap,
> For in my way it lies. Stars, hide your fires,
> Let not light see my black and deep desires;   (1.4.50–53)

This speech depicts the crucial moment of Macbeth's commitment to the deed, long before Lady Macbeth enters the scene. Macbeth has clear reason to envy Malcolm if he is to believe the logic of the witches' prophecy, but that logic is itself an expression of the murderous economy of competition that the rebellion has encouraged in the kingdom. The essence of the speech is its categorical and inverse reasoning: "I must fall down, or else o'erleap"—an image that anticipates Macbeth's subsequent reference to "Vaulting ambition which o'erleaps itself" (1.7.27)—and this reasoning is in turn the expression of the dark and aspiring desires that both Augustine and Freud find to be at the source of human infirmity and guilt, and that Montaigne, less homiletically, sees as a natural basis of human conduct. As Coleridge suggests,[18] Milton seems to be evoking this moment in the play (and an Augustinian interpretation of it) when he describes how Satan,

> fraught
> With envy against the Son of God, that day
> Honoured by his great Father, and proclaimed
> Messiah king anointed, could not bear
> Through pride that sight, and thought himself impaired.
>
> (PL 5:661–65)

Macbeth's pride and envy are not dissimilar, and his own sense of impairment is conveyed in a number of ways in the play. The most basic is both his and our constant sense that his parricidal quest is necessarily unattainable, a fantasy beyond the reach of reality. A very young boy may wish in his imagination to take his father's place, but he obviously cannot do so in fact. He literally cannot perform his father's role, either sexually or in other ways, and in this respect such childhood fantasies are like the drunken lust the Porter describes, only far more frightening. Macbeth always knows this. Lady Macbeth at first does not. She herself explicitly recognizes the parricidal impetus behind the murder of Duncan, but though that recognition both deters and eventually destroys her, its most immediate effect seems to be to excite her.

Macbeth never experiences such excitement and is always "bound in" by fear because in him is represented that part of a childhood sensibility that always understands the enterprise to be physically impossible. The play's celebrated clothing images, and their precise development in the course of the action, make this part of Macbeth's predicament unusually clear. Banquo, when speaking of the new honors that have come to Macbeth, refers to "strange garments" that "cleave not to their mould / But with the aid of use" (1.3.144–45), but Banquo looks into the "seeds of time" (1.3.56) and is willing to let them grow. Macbeth, on the other hand, like a child, cannot wait, and the garments to which he aspires will never fit him: early in the play he calls them "borrowed robes" (1.3.107), later they are called the dress of his drunken hopes, and finally they "Hang loose about him, like a giant's robe / Upon a dwarfish thief" (5.2.21–22). That final description has many reverberations. In his discussion of the enviousness and "tantrums" of infants in the *Confessions*,

Augustine remarks that "it is the weaknes of Infants bodyes, which are innocent, wheras their mind is not innocent." [19] The image of Macbeth as a dwarf in giant's clothes in part suggests the horrifying marriage of an infant's mind with adult strength; but the purely physical impact of the image also underlines the impotence of such a union, for in the last analysis Macbeth simply cannot fill the role and title to which he aspires. He is called a dwarf rather than a child because he has indeed exercised terrifying adult powers, but what the image nonetheless finally suggests is the radical disproportion between a small child and the grown-up man he wishes all at once to replace and become.

This sense of disproportion, if not disjunction, is central to the entire play. The Porter points to the obvious sexual manifestation of disjunction, in discriminating the gap between drunken desire and performance, but his speech is itself only a part of the prevailing concern in the play with the larger and deeper relationship between thought and action. That relationship is Macbeth's own single most constant and important preoccupation, and, as suggested earlier, its roots can be traced to the infantile world of magical thinking, the stage of human development in which the self is all-encompassing. This stage is an absolute realization of Macbeth's metaphor of the "single state of man," for to an infant his own body and the world's body seem coextensive, and the microcosm and the macrocosm are experienced as one. External reality for an infant, Freud maintained, is composed of his own sensations and the projection, often hallucinatory, of his own wishes and fears—of his "thoughts"—and because these thoughts can ignore the coordinates of time and space, "since what lies furthest apart both in time and space can without difficulty be comprehended in a single act of consciousness," they seem omnipotent. [20] Freud suggests in *Totem and Taboo* that this infantile narcissism is the source of animism and that it actually characterized primitive man, who practiced magic and peopled the universe with spirits, who "knew what things were like in the world, namely just as he felt himself to be," who "transposed the structural conditions of his own mind into the external world." [21] "In the animistic epoch," Freud remarks, "the reflection of the internal world is bound to blot out the other picture of the world—the one which *we* seem to perceive." [22] He also argues that such animistic thinking is still present in more civilized and adult experience, in the very nature of dreamwork as well as in more conscious life. Its more beneficent or paradisal residues he finds in the state of being in love, when against the normal evidence of external reality, the lovers feel the "I" and "thou" to be one; its more malign and hellish traces he finds in the behavior of neurotics and psychotics in whom the formation of symptoms is determined by "the reality not of experience but of thought," who "live in a world apart," who "are only affected by what is thought with intensity and pictured with emotion." [23]

A. P. Rossiter writes that in *Macbeth* Shakespeare represents "the passionate will-to-self-assertion, to unlimited self-hood, and especially the impulsion to force the world (and everything in it) to *my* pattern, in *my* time, and with my own hand." [24] I think that Rossiter is correct and that behind this "will" and "impulsion," whose force in the play he himself finds somewhat puzzling, is the whole realm of primitive narcissism in which Macbeth is "cabined, cribbed, confined" and with which the entire action of the play resonates, a realm in which there is no past or future except what is pictured as being fulfilled in the present, in the moment of thought. Lady Macbeth suggests the character of such magical thought and its childhood origins quite precisely when she rebukes Macbeth for his unwillingness to face Duncan's dead body:

> The sleeping and the dead,
> Are but as pictures. 'Tis the eye of childhood
> That fears a painted devil.   (2.2.51–53)

The reference to "pictures" is especially suggestive because visual images, which are the language of infancy and childhood, are also the language of dreams, and they constitute not only the substance of Macbeth's nightmare thoughts, but often his impetus to action. [25]

Though Lady Macbeth correctly locates the "eye of childhood" in Macbeth's consciousness, the primitive world of magical and animistic thinking, like the filaments of parricidal competition, pervades the whole play as well. Metaphorical analogies between the macrocosm and microcosm are constant and have unusual power in *Macbeth*, and as A. C. Bradley and most subsequent critics have recognized, the fearful state of mind within Macbeth and the state of Scotland outside of him seem often indistinguishable. Equally important, nature itself is literally animated in the play—most conspicuously when Birnam Wood indeed moves to Dunsinane—and the play is filled with suggestions of actual magic. There is white magic in the "good" English king, who has "a heavenly gift of prophecy" and whose hand and "healing benediction" can cure "the disease . . . call'd the evil" (4.3.147 ff.); and black magic, of course, is represented in the witches. Macbeth does not create the witches, and we see them before he does. They open the play and establish its environment before Macbeth ever appears, and when he himself sees them, so does Banquo. Banquo does not, like Macbeth, become obsessed with them, but he does nonetheless respond to the magical potency of the realm of thought they represent. Both men wonder (in much the same way that Macbeth will later wonder about his hallucinations) whether the witches are real. Banquo asks, "Are ye fantastical or that indeed / Which outwardly ye show?" (1.3.51–52), and Macbeth says that "what seemed corporal / Melted as breath into the wind" (1.3.79–80). Though the witches eventually come to seem more exclusively the projection of Macbeth's own mind, they are never only that, and they are always corporeal for us as well as him. Their presence hardly exonerates Macbeth of his crimes, but it does encourage imaginative sympathy with him, for their powerful effect onstage necessarily draws an audience into the realm of magical and hallucinatory thinking of which they are so palpable an expression.

It is nonetheless within Macbeth's own consciousness that this realm has its most profound and compelling representation in the play. All Shakespearean tragic heroes "live in a world apart," but none so clearly and completely in "the reality not of experience but of thought," in an "internal world" of hallucinations and apparitions that "blot[s] out the other picture of the world—the one which *we* seem to perceive," an internal world of fearful and "fantastical" thought in which, in Macbeth's own words, "function is smother'd in surmise / And nothing is but what is not." The Renaissance conception of the passion of fear, the passion to which Lady Macbeth refers when she speaks of a "painted devil," is peculiarly apposite to Macbeth. In *Of Wisedome* Pierre Charron writes that since fear "serves it[s] turne with that which is to come, where though we seeme to foresee much, we see nothing at all," it holds us in "doubtfull darkness . . . as in a darke place":

> feare seemeth not to other end, than to make us finde
> that which we flie from. Doubtlesse, feare is of all other
> evils the greatest and most tedious: for other evils are no
> longer evils than they continue, and the paine endureth
> no longer than the cause; but feare is of that which is,
> and that which is not, and that perhaps which shall
> never be, yea sometimes of that which can not possible
> be. Beholde then a passion truly malicious and tyranni-
> call, which draweth from an imaginarie evill true and
> bitter sorrowes, and is over-greedie by thought and opin-
> ion to overtake, nay out-run them.[26]

Macbeth's effort to predict the future in a literally dark world; his finding what he flies from and his fearing what is not, as well as what is; his subjection to a tyrannical passion that extends outward to his subjects as well as inward to his own soul; his overgreediness of thought: the passage speaks almost in Macbeth's own language.

Charron in effect describes a regression to primitive, if not animistic, thinking. Macbeth's fear is particularly compelling because he has an acute and adult awareness of his regressive thoughts and their nature. Indeed, it is the very awareness of such thoughts that he ultimately dreads most and that most torments him. It is the fear behind his fears. Macbeth's characteristic posture, virtually a physical posture onstage, is isolated self-absorption, in manifold senses of the term. He is first "rapt" (1.3.55) then quickly literally "lost" in his "thoughts" (2.2.69–70), not only in soliloquies, in which such preoccupation is conventional, but in the midst of communal occasions, the banquet being the most memorable (and where the apparition that causes his fear and withdrawal seems more purely the creation of his own mind). More important, the thoughts in which he is lost, the "scorpions" with which his mind is full (3.2.37), are usually not only about himself, but about the very pressure of thought in his consciousness, and most specifically about the urgent need to make the thoughts deeds and thereby terminate them—in his own repeated words, to make the hand and heart one.[27] In *The Rape of Lucrece*, interestingly, Tarquin exhibits the same tyranny of thought and the same animistic impulse to conflate what he sees outside himself with what he feels within himself: "My heart," he says, "shall never countermand mine eye" (276). This need perhaps suggests the fear of disintegration that in part energizes animistic thinking. This fear is hinted at in Tarquin, but it is expressed most fully in Macbeth—in his persistent anxiety that parts of his body are becoming separated from each other and in the dread and urgency of his quest to bring them absolutely together in his mind.

Lady Macbeth touches directly upon these feelings in her attack on Macbeth's manhood. She says, when he hesitates to kill Duncan,

> Art thou afeard
> To be the same in thine own act and valour
> As thou art in desire? . . .
> When you durst do it, then you were a man;
> And to be more than what you were, you would
> Be so much more the man. (1.7.39–41, 49–51)

These lines, which anticipate the Porter's, reflect the parricidal motifs of the play, but they also suggest the more primal realm of self-love that lies behind Macbeth's quest to "transpose the structural conditions of his own mind into the external world." This quest takes two forms: altering the perception of reality within his own mind and altering external reality to conform to his thoughts. The effort in either case is pathological and destructive, and Lady Macbeth shows its eventual outcome in actual life by collapsing and withdrawing entirely into a hallucinatory world of sleepwalking.

The alteration of Macbeth's own consciousness is first suggested in the raptness with which he meditates upon the witches' prophecy, but it is most decisively presented in the soliloquy that describes his hallucination of the bloody dagger. He recognizes that he is seeing "a dagger of the mind, a false creation / Proceeding from the heat-oppressèd brain," and concludes with clarity that "There's no such thing. / It is the bloody business which informs / Thus to mine eyes" (2.1.38–39, 47–49). The final effect of the soliloquy, however, is to represent Macbeth's dread of disintegration and the consequent need for hallucination in order literally to compose himself, the need for his "eyes" to be "made the fools o'th' other senses, / Or else worth all the rest" (2.1.44–45).

At the end of the soliloquy Macbeth seems to recover his composure—he seems, again literally, to pull himself together—and his thoughts appear to turn outward:

> Thou sure and firm-set earth,
> Hear not my steps which way they walk, for fear
> Thy very stones prate of my whereabout,
> And take the present horror from the time,
> Which now suits with it.   (2.1.56–60)

These lines are difficult but also typical of Macbeth. They suggest not only, as J. Dover Wilson remarks, that Macbeth "speaks as if watching himself in a dream,"[28] but specifically that Macbeth wants the outer scene to express the inner one, as it does in dreamwork, that after resisting the impulse to imagine a reality created by and within his own thoughts, he is now preparing to transform the external world to make it conform to those thoughts. The whole of the speech represents Macbeth's utter unwillingness to tolerate any division between what is outside and what is inside himself, and his cold closing lines forecast the ruthlessness with which he will attempt to make the two consonant: "Whiles I threat, he lives. / Words to the heat of deeds too cold breath gives" (2.1.60–61).

Macbeth's murder of Duncan is his first attempt to bring about such a consonance: in parricidal terms by making himself sole sovereign of his world, the one and only; and on the more primal level of narcissism by making himself and his kingdom coextensive, by literalizing the metaphor of the king's two bodies. Lady Macbeth, appropriately, plays a major part in the parricidal aspiration, but the conscious pursuit of the more primal quest is Macbeth's alone, and it intensifies after the murder of Duncan, as he successively plans the destruction of Banquo and Fleance and of Macduff's family without Lady Macbeth's knowledge.

In contemplating the first of these family murders, Macbeth says:

> For mine own good,
> All causes shall give way. I am in blood
> Stepped in so far that, should I wade no more,
> Returning were as tedious as go o'er.
> Strange things I have in head that will to hand,
> Which must be acted ere they may be scanned. (3.4.134–39)

The distance—in time if not in space—between head and hand is nearly gone when he conceives the murder of Macduff's family. Informed that Macduff has gone to England, he says:

> Time, thou anticipat'st my dread exploits.
> The flighty purpose never is o'ertook
> Unless the deed go with it. From this moment
> The very firstlings of my heart shall be
> The firstlings of my hand. And even now,
> To crown my thoughts with acts, be it thought and done.
>
> (4.1.160–65)

This is the crown to which Macbeth has aspired all along—to be, in Lady Macbeth's words, "transported . . . beyond / This ignorant present" and "feel . . . The future in the instant" (1.5.55–57), to have the omnipotent power to contain the whole world

within his own mind and to make it entirely in his own image—
to be, as Augustine says man wished to be at the Fall, and as he
is in his mind in infancy, like a god. The moment is the apogee
of his ambition. It is also the turning point in the action. Unburdened of the gap between the heart and the hand, the thought
and the act, the present and the future, he loses the energy of
his fear—"I have almost forgot the taste of fears. . . . Direness,
familiar to my slaughterous thoughts, / Cannot once start me"
(5.5.9, 14–15)—but without the distinction between himself
and the outside world, and without the future, he also begins to
lose the energy and definition of life itself. "Tomorrow" becomes
a meaningless prolongation of today, and he becomes "aweary of
the sun" (5.5.18–19, 47). And as he begins to lose life, the outside world begins to regain it. Macbeth's crowning of his thoughts
is followed by the slaughter of Lady Macduff and her child, but
also immediately afterward by the scene in which Malcolm successfully tests Macduff: Malcolm states that his "thoughts cannot
transpose" Macduff's inner nature (4.3.22), but he nonetheless
learns to "know" Macduff through an imitation of Macbeth that
is also an exorcism of Macbeth's world of transposing thoughts.

Montaigne describes such a world of thought very interestingly in his essay entitled "Of Judging of Others Death." He remarks that we all see the world as an extension of our own
individual existence and that this irreducible self-absorption
leads us to believe the universe has the "same motion" we do:
"Forsomuch as our sight being altered, represents unto it selfe
things alike; and we imagine, that things faile it, as it doth to
them: As they who travell by Sea, to whom mountaines, fields,
townes, heaven and earth, seeme to goe the same motion, and
keepe the same course, they doe." He associates this way of
thinking most particularly with the fear of death and concludes
that "no one of us thinkes it sufficient, to be but one."[29] All of
Shakespeare's greatest tragic heroes have the infantile presumption Montaigne describes—none of them can be said to think it
sufficient to be but one. Macbeth's presumptuous thinking, however, is both more radical than and different from that of other
Shakespearean heroes in a way that is important and instructive.
Lear's need, for example, to imagine that heaven and earth move

as he does is indeed an infantile denial of his mortal limits, as he himself intermittently realizes—"They told me I was everything; 'tis a lie, I am not ague-proof" (4.5.104–5). But Lear regresses into infancy because old people naturally do so and because he is afraid of dying. He protests against death, in the last analysis, because he wants to hold on to life and its real human relationships, particularly, at the end, to the love of his child Cordelia. In *Macbeth*, however, "All is the fear and nothing is the love" (4.2.12), and Macbeth's attempt to make the world keep to his motion is essentially a flight from human relationships and a denial not of death but of life. For his fear of the distance between his thoughts and the world outside of them is finally a fear of consciousness itself; and his regression to the inordinate self-love of primary narcissism is a return to the "perfect" safety and "perfect" integrity of the womb, which, as Rosse says of Macbeth's Scotland, "cannot / Be called our mother, but our grave" (4.3.166–67).

It is common to say that Macbeth's ambition is suicidal. It may be more exact and revealing to recognize that nonbeing is his ambition, that he commits himself from the first to the suicide that Lady Macbeth acts out at the end, that his deepest wish is to annihilate the very self he asserts. This acute paradox is adumbrated with almost allegorical clarity earlier in Shakespeare's career in *Richard III*. In the first part of the play, while he is still climbing, Richard III is untroubled—like the medieval Vice with whom he explicitly allies himself, he is singularly "motivated," joyous in the humor and histrionics of his intrigues, the unalloyed, if destructive energy of the aspiring will. But once he attains the throne and that energy cannot be directed outwards, it is turned against himself, and he seems immediately deflated. He confesses that "I have not that alacrity of spirit, / Nor cheer of mind, that I was wont to have" (5.5.26–27), and after he awakens from his dream on Bosworth Field, he realizes that his love of himself is now destroying him:

What do I fear? Myself? There's none else by.
Richard loves Richard; that is, I am I.

Is there a murderer here? No. Yes, I am.
Then fly! What, from myself? Great reason. Why?
Lest I revenge. Myself upon myself?
Alack, I love myself. Wherefore? For any good
That I myself have done unto myself?
O no, alas, I rather hate myself
For hateful deeds committed by myself. . . .
I shall despair. There is no creature loves me,
And if I die no soul will pity me.
Nay, wherefore should they?—Since that I myself
Find in myself no pity to myself.   (5.5.136–44, 154–57)

The sense of astonishment in this implosive speech is perhaps
more than Richard's alone. Richard appreciably changes in these
lines from a personification into a man, and the speech suggests
Shakespeare's own discovery of the dramatic potential of transposing the allegorical topography of the morality drama into the
consciousness of a single individual. But in any case the soliloquy
precisely discriminates the suicidal paradox of Richard's quest to
be, as he says in another context, "myself alone" (3 Henry VI,
5.6.84), and it anticipates the tremendous force of that paradox
in the tragedy of Macbeth.

The apparent contradiction that Richard sees with such clarity—"Myself upon myself? / Alack, I love myself"—can be explained in complementary Augustinian and Freudian terms. For
Augustine, self-love, the soul's desire to be its own beginner, to
be everything, both results in and is born of emptiness, of nothingness. The Freudian analogue is the self-love of primary narcissism. Echoes of such narcissism exist in all human beings, and in
an infant the condition is natural. The regression to such a condition in an adult, however, is truly to confound Hell in Elysium,
for except in the state of intense love in which the self is paradoxically at once lost and aggrandized, the godlike presumption
of primary narcissism results in a sense only of the loss of the
self, because a self that encompasses everything ultimately cannot be defined by anything, and is indeed defined by nothing.
The premise common to both the Augustinian and the Freudian

conception is that human beings must exist in relation to a reality outside themselves, that, as Wallace Stevens observes, "nothing is itself taken alone. Things are because of interrelations and interactions." [30]

The Augustinian reverberations of Macbeth's tragedy are explicit and emphatic. Among Macbeth's first words after he has achieved the crown are, "To be thus is nothing" (3.1.49); both he and Lady Macbeth immediately yearn to join the safety and "peace" of the man they have murdered (3.2.8, 22); and the subsequent action progresses inevitably toward the state of mind in which Macbeth sees all of life as

> a tale
> Told by an idiot, full of sound and fury
> Signifying nothing   (5.5.25–27)

and toward its counterpart in the literal suicide of his wife. What distinguishes *Macbeth* from *Richard III* in this respect is not only that Macbeth is partially conscious of the movement toward nothing from the beginning (as Richard is not), but that the whole play, and particularly the relationship of Macbeth and Lady Macbeth, dramatizes the emotional character of that movement more fully. A sense of emotional emptiness permeates the play. Lady Macbeth expresses it explicitly soon after the killing of Duncan when she speaks of attaining desire "without content" and of spending all and having "naught"; and it informs Macbeth's actions throughout, in the undercurrent of weariness even in his earlier soliloquies, and in the appalling tedium of feeling and spirit that he exhibits in contemplating his later homicides.

Underlying this emotional emptiness, as well as expressing it, is the same deep sense of self-division that emerges at the end of *Richard III*. The equivocations that flood the language and action of *Macbeth* are one expression of such division, and Macbeth, of course, depicts it directly: in his continuous indecision early in the play; in the collocation of aspiration and dread in his consciousness until nearly the end of the play; and even at the end, when he seems beyond fear, in his sleeplessness, a sleeplessness that is at once a denial, to use his own words, of "great nature's second course, / Chief nourisher in life's feast" and a protection against "The death of each day's life" (2.2.37–38, 36).

But the most compelling representation of self-division and ultimately of self-alienation in the play is the relationship between Macbeth and Lady Macbeth that constitutes the central dramatic interest of the play. For the two of them do, as Freud observes, suggest disunited parts of a single psychic entity, and Shakespeare literalizes this psychomachic conception in a way that accentuates Macbeth's and Lady Macbeth's deprivation not only as husband and wife but also as individuals. For though they may constitute a whole allegorically, literally they never can "complete" each other. Shakespeare at once symbiotically connects and permanently dissevers them. Early in the play Lady Macbeth relishes the thought of murdering Duncan, while Macbeth dreads it; later she retreats from thoughts of killing, while he embraces them. He, at the start, seems without will, while she seems defined by it (though, interestingly, her will can be expressed only through her husband, for whom she has contempt, so that the being composed by the two of them suggests self-hatred as well as self-love from the start); as the play proceeds, his willpower seems to increase in inverse proportion to the diminishment of hers; and by the end their positions are reversed, she becoming "all remorse and he all defiance."[31] The cumulative effect of such oppositions and inversions—and many more could be elaborated, since they draw upon all the antinomies of parricide and narcissism in the play—is to suggest not so much change, or even conflict, within the composite soul of Macbeth and Lady Macbeth, as stasis and atrophy. For the more the various terms of the division between Macbeth and Lady Macbeth are inverted, the more they remain the same. The result is not only an increasing sense of the soul's paralysis and depletion of energy, but a sense that between the unchanging terms of the division is indeed "nothing," a void.

Macbeth's reference to the nourishment that his sleeplessness denies him has a counterpart in the lines of Lady Macbeth that refer to the primal image of life's nourishment, and her speech suggests how elemental is the emptiness that the two of them incarnate:

> I have given suck, and know
> How tender 'tis to love the babe that milks me.
> I would, while it was smiling in my face,
> Have plucked my nipple from his boneless gums,
> And dash'd the brains out, had I so sworn
> As you have done to this.   (1.7.54–59)

This is the root of the many images in *Macbeth* of murdered children and of naked, newborn, and bloody babies,[32] and it is the "rooted sorrow" (5.3.43) not only of Lady Macbeth but of the whole tragedy. The deepest forms of despair are often traced to the deprivation of maternal nourishment. The image, as well as the actuality, of a mother's nurture of an infant at her breast is the irreducible basis of human development—the "rock" upon which the first sense of the self must be "founded," the "casing air" that nourishes the "broad and general" promise of all subsequent relationships (3.4.21, 22). *Macbeth* is so bleak and horrifying an experience because it presents a world in which this foundation and promise are violated. For what Lady Macbeth imagines, Macbeth enacts. His attempt, in Augustine's words, to be his own beginner and his insatiable hunger for more and more can be understood as a desperate effort to fill the void she describes, but it is also and necessarily a movement backwards and downwards toward it; and in that regressive quest and movement toward nothingness, he denies the creative processes and relationships that nourish and renew life and give it meaning. Like Night in *The Rape of Lucrece* and the night that envelops this play, he "Make[s] war against proportioned course of time" (774). Childless and a grotesque conflation of child and adult himself, he wishes to level the distinction between the two in all others. He kills the old and the young, fathers and children and, at his extremity, a mother and child.

All of Shakespeare's tragic heroes move toward death, the formal as well as defining end of their dramas, but in no other play is that movement so willfully life-denying, and for this reason *Macbeth* seems the least redemptive of Shakespeare's great

tragedies. There is a disposition among recent critics and direc-
tors of the play also to find it fundamentally problematic, to
stress, for example, the endemic and latently murderous competition within the whole world of the play as well as the absence
of effective feminine values and the ultimate emptiness of
all that defines courage and manliness. But this is to treat the
play as if it were an argument and to grasp a point and miss it
at the same time, for *Macbeth* is a tragedy of the deliberate
emptying out of human life, and as in all the tragedies, and
in this one above all, the condition of the hero becomes and
is the condition of the world that both Shakespeare and he
create in his image. In the tragic world of *Macbeth*, to be a hero
is to enact the human consequences of the predicament of
Satan, for whom also, in Milton's words, "the mind is its own
place," "not to be changed by place or time" (*PL* 1:254, 253).
Shakespeare makes us experience the tragic passion of such a
"place," because we are made to see so much through Macbeth's
eyes, but that experience is itself a function of our awareness,
no less than his, of the values that his demonic thoughts seek
to deny. There is always a syncopation of sympathy and judgment in our response to him. We always understand in the play
that human beings, unlike devils, cannot respire without the
changes of time and place and the related hierarchies of human
generation and nurture, that our individual identity as well
as our common humanity depends upon our willingness to
give to and receive from others. We can so deeply participate
in the hell Macbeth creates and inhabits precisely because
the play makes us apprehend and feel these truths, because
we always know, as he increasingly does, what is absent,
"what," truly, "is not." Our essential experience, like his, is the
pain of loss.

The nature of this loss is represented everywhere in the play,
but it is most crystallized in the scenes and speeches that emphasize human relationships and human community. It is shown in
the peculiar horror of Macbeth's isolation during the banquet
scene—the scene Simon Forman remembered most—and it is
stated explicitly by Macbeth when he laments that

> that which should accompany old age,
> As honour, love, obedience, troops of friends,
> I must not look to have.   (5.3.26–28)

And it is asserted most profoundly in the experience of Macduff. Macduff is not a hero, but he is Macbeth's proper nemesis. His not being "of woman born" suggests, I think, more about Macbeth's thinking than his own,[33] but it also perhaps frees him from the profound terror of the regressive movement Macbeth has imposed upon the world of the play. Macduff alone in Scotland seems unafraid to know himself and is therefore the one most concerned for others. It is fitting that it is he who announces at the end of the play, in words that touch upon the depths of Macbeth's tragedy, that "the time is free" (5.11.21). Some critics, as well as contemporary productions like Roman Polanski's film version of the play, suggest that the announcement is overconfident and that the play's ending, like its beginning, is equivocal and implicates Macduff (among others) in the same ethos of blood as Macbeth's. Macduff admittedly leaves his family unprotected, and he submits, in the midst of his grief over their loss, to Malcolm's call for vengeance. And, not without savagery of his own, he too kills a king. But to contend that he thereby "steps into [Macbeth's] role"[34] and becomes his double is to devalue the play's real equivocations and ironies and to pursue modern shibboleths of contradiction and inversion at the expense not only of what is manifest but also of what deeply moves us. Whatever else we may feel about Lady Macduff's pain and bewilderment at Macduff's absence, we know that she is incorrect in thinking that he has taken "flight" and that his "fears" have prompted him (4.2.3–4). Macduff leaves his family as a soldier goes to war, out of duty to his whole society. He does not anticipate, because he cannot imagine, the wantonness of the murder of his wife and children, and the guilt that he assumes for their death includes the one he shares with all mankind (4.3.226). Lady Macduff's cry "All is the fear and nothing is the love" (4.2.12) is, for us, a description of the Macbeths, not of Macduff.[35] And though Macduff's role in the play is certainly to kill Macbeth, it is grief that prompts him, and it is his grief that we remember. If he lets that grief "convert to anger" and "enrage his heart" (4.3.230), as Malcolm urges, he has cause, and we ourselves respond to that rage not as a symptom of emotional impoverishment but, on the contrary, as an expression of the fullness of his sorrow. When Malcolm tells him to "dispute" his grief "like a man," Macduff answers:

> I shall do so,
> But I must also feel it as a man.
> I cannot but remember such things were
> That were most precious to me.   (4.3.221–25)

It is no accident that these painful lines should bring into focus what it really means to be a man, and a comparison with Macbeth's atrophied response to the death of his own wife is inescapable: "She should have died hereafter. / There would have been a time for such a word" (5.5.16–17).

There is never any doubt in this play how much is lost and what is lost in Macbeth's primitive quest for his "own good."

CHAPTER V

KING LEAR

THE EXPERIENCE OF FEELING—feeling that is physical as well as emotional—is at the core of *King Lear*, as the enlargement of our own capacity to feel is at the core of any persuasive explanation of why we can take pleasure in such a tragedy. The tragedy raises the largest of metaphysical issues, but as in *Hamlet*, it is the "heart-struck injuries" (3.1.8) that give rise to such questions upon which Shakespeare focuses and to which we are compelled to respond. Hamlet speaks of the "heartache" of human existence. In *King Lear* we hear of and then see hearts "cracked" (2.1.89) and "split" (5.3.168). Edgar tells us that his father died when his "flawed heart . . . 'Twixt two extremes of passion, joy and grief, / Burst smilingly" (5.3.188, 190–91), and at the moment of Lear's death, Kent says, "Break, heart, I prithee break." (5.3.288), a line that confirms the truth of what we have just witnessed, whether it refers to Lear's heart or to Kent's own.

The dramatization of the metaphor of a breaking heart and its association with the extremity of dying itself are critical to *King Lear*, for though, again like *Hamlet*, *King Lear's* essential preoccupation is with the anguish of living in the face of death, it does not, like the earlier play, look beyond the grave. It focuses instead, and relentlessly, upon the fractured heart and upon actual human decomposition—the physical "eyes' anguish" (4.5.6) of Gloucester's maiming, the emotional "eye of anguish" (4.3.15) of Lear's madness. And the fifth act of the play brings no relief, as it does in *Hamlet*. There is no recovery from sorrow and grief at the end of *Lear*, nor is there even a glimpse of the "special providence" that Hamlet sees in the fall of a sparrow. Lear's question over Cordelia's lifeless body, "Why should a dog, a horse, a rat have life, / And thou no breath at all?" (5.3.282–83) is not answered in the play, certainly not by his own few succeeding words; and among those words the ones that are most unequivocal and that we most remember are: "Thou'lt come no more. / Never, never, never, never, never." (5.3.283–84) These lines express the immediate feeling of all of us in the presence of the death and dying of those we love, but they have an intensified and governing power in *King Lear*. They occur at the very end, they occur after protracted suffering, they violate the hopes that appear to be raised by the reunion of Lear and Cordelia, and they occur over the dead body of a character who seems to symbolize the heart's imperishable resources of love in the play. There is no scene in Shakespeare that represents the wrench of death more absolutely or more painfully; and the scene is not merely the conclusion of the action of the play, it is its recapitulation, the moment in which the whole of it is crystallized.

In this respect, as in others, *King Lear* seems very reminiscent of Ecclesiastes. The depiction of suffering in the play has often been compared to that in the Book of Job.[1] Job, of course, focuses upon an individual, and the protraction of Job's suffering as well as his protests against it suggest the magnitude of Lear's heroic characterization, as Ecclesiastes does not. But there is no Satan at the beginning of *King Lear* nor a whirlwind from which God speaks at the end to make the play's extraordinary sense of heartfelt pain even intellectually explicable. In its overall conception as well as in much of its ironic texture, *King Lear* is closer to Ecclesiastes, the book of the Old Testament that condemns the world so severely as to be nearly pagan in its outlook and that treats human life almost exclusively, and despairingly, in terms of the immanence of its ending.

The Preacher in Ecclesiastes speaks over and over again of the heart, occasionally of the "heart of the wise" or "of fooles" (7:6), but most often of his own: "And I have given mine heart to search & finde out wisdome" (1:13); "I thoght in mine heart" (1:16); "And I gave mine heart" (1:17); "I said in mine heart" (2:1); "I soght in mine heart" (2:3). The Preacher's experience of the heart suggests many of the major motifs as well as the specific language of *King Lear*. His announced theme is "vanity," a word which is glossed in the Geneva Bible as "nothing" and which the New English Bible translates as "emptiness," and he speaks of man's identity in this life as "a shadow" (7:2) and his achievements as "nothing" (5:14, 7:16). He compares men to beasts: "For the condition of the children of men, and the condition of beasts are even as one condition unto them. As the one dyeth, so dyeth the other: for they have all one breath, and there is no excellencie of man above the beast: for all is vanitie" (3:19). He speaks of man's nakedness: "As he came forthe of his mothers belly, he shal returne naked to go as he came, & shal beare away nothing of his labour, which he hathe caused to passe by his hand" (5:14). He talks constantly of the paradoxes of wisdom and folly and madness: "And I gave mine heart to knowe wisdome & knowledge, madnes & foolishnes: I knew also that this is a vexacion of the spirit. / For in the multitude of wisdome is muche grief: & he that encreaseth knowledge, encreaseth sorowe" (1:17–18). He associates such paradoxes with kingship: "Better is a poore and wise childe, then an olde and foolish King, which wil no more be admonished" (4:13), and he associates them as well with eyesight: "For the wise man's eyes *are* in his head, but the foole walketh in darkenes: yet I know also that the same condition falleth to them all" (2:14). He also associates "the sight of the eye" with "lustes" (6:9) and he speaks of how men are killed like fishes in a net and birds in a snare (9:12). And he meditates upon the paradoxes of justice and injustice: "I have sene all things in the daies of my vanitie: there is a juste man that perisheth in his justice, and there is a wicked man that continueth long in his malice" (7:17). "There is a vanitie, which is done upon the earth, that there be righteous men to whome it cometh according to the worke of the wicked: and there be wicked men to whome it cometh according to the juste: I thoght also that this is vanitie" (8:14). The premise as well as the conclusion of all these experiences is that "all things *come* to all alike:

and the same condition *is* to the juste and to the wicked, to the good and to the pure, & to the polluted, & to him that sacrificeth, & to him that sacrificeth not: as *is* the good, so *is* the sinner, he that sweareth, as he that feareth an othe" (9:2).

These verses suggest many analogues to *King Lear:* the old and foolish King; the paradoxes of folly and wisdom that occupy the Fool's speeches and songs; the dramatization of the metaphors of sight in Gloucester's whole characterization; the nakedness of birth and death and of man's whole condition that is lamented by Lear and palpably represented in Edgar; the random wantonness of death of which Gloucester complains; the comparisons of men and beasts which suffuse the language of the play and which are especially prominent in Lear's speeches, including his last; the vision of the confluence of the just and the wicked that consumes Lear on the heath and that leads him to conclude, not unlike the Preacher, that "None does offend, none, I say none" (4.5.164).

Shakespeare could have absorbed, and no doubt did absorb, each of these preoccupations from sources other than Ecclesiastes, notably from Montaigne's "Apologie of *Raymond Sebond*," [2] as well as from the Bible itself, including its descriptions of the end of the world. [3] The vision of the Apocalypse in Mark 13, for example, virtually describes the central action of *King Lear:* "There shal rise nation against nation, & kingdome against kingdome: and there shal be earthquakes . . . the brother shall betray the brother to death, and the father the sonne: and the children shal rise against their fathers and mothers, and shal put them to death." But if the Apocalypse suggests the general social and political chaos of *Lear,* the world of Ecclesiastes too was traditionally understood to be portrayed in the implicit context of the Last Judgment, and the large number of evocations of Ecclesiastes (and many more could be cited) gives that chaos its emotional definition. The Preacher's lament that "he that encreaseth knowledge, encreaseth sorowe" is a line the Fool could sing: it has the cadence as well as the substance of his whole characterization and its relationship with Lear's. The Preacher's repeated references to the anguish of his own heart suggest the pain of protest as well as of resignation, a combination of feelings that

King Lear eventually also elicits—in us, if not also, at the last, in Lear himself. And perhaps most important, if most obvious, *vanitas*, the theme which echoes endlessly in Ecclesiastes and which *King Lear* catches up in its preoccupation with the word *nothing*, leads not just to the notion of emptiness, but to its paradoxically full feeling, the feeling to which Edgar refers at the end when he says that we should "Speak what we feel, not what we ought to say" (5.3.300). The feeling has a far greater amplitude and richness in the play than in Ecclesiastes, but its roots are the same.

What underlies all of these motifs is the focus upon death as the universal event in human existence that not only ends life but calls its whole meaning into question. At one point in Ecclesiastes the Preacher asks, "Who is as the wise man? and who knoweth the interpretacion of a thing?" (8:1), and the burden of the question is that given the transience and mutability of human life, who *can* know? As in *King Lear*, which also asks this question insistently, there is no satisfying answer, and certainly no consoling one. But again like *Lear*, Ecclesiastes does offer a characteristic perception of human existence in the face of death, if not an interpretation of it. For the Preacher's anguished sense of the dissolution of all things in time almost necessarily impels him to think of those things in terms of polarities—the polarities of beginnings and endings especially, but also of their cognates in creativeness and destructiveness—and to think of life itself as a composition of extremes that have individual moral definition but are not necessarily morally intelligible as a whole. He suggests this understanding in the passage already quoted in which he says that "all things come alike to all," to the just and the wicked, the good and the pure, and that "as *is* the good, so *is* the sinner," and he does so strikingly in the passage for which Ecclesiastes is now best known and which is regularly cited in liturgies for the dead, the passage that speaks of a time to be born and a time to die, a time to slay and a time to heal, to weep and to laugh, to seek and to lose, to keep and to cast away, to be silent and to speak, to love and to hate (3:1–8).

This landscape of antinomies suggests the deepest of the affinities between Ecclesiastes and *King Lear*, for the kingdom of *Lear* too is defined by the antinomy of "coming hither" and "going hence" (5.2.10) and by corresponding polarizations of human states of feeling and being. The association of such contrasts with the experience of death is adumbrated earlier in Shakespeare's career in *Richard II*, a play that is also concerned with an abdication that is a prefiguration of death:

> What must the King do now? Must he submit?
> The King shall do it. Must he be deposed?
> The King shall be contented. Must he lose
> The name of King? A God's name, let it go.
> I'll give my jewels for a set of beads,
> My gorgeous palace for a hermitage,
> My gay apparel for an almsman's gown,
> My figured goblets for a dish of wood,
> My sceptre for a palmer's walking staff,
> My subjects for a pair of carved saints,
> And my large kingdom for a little grave
> A little, little grave, an obscure grave. (*Richard II*, 3.3.142–53)[4]

Richard's itemization of these oppositions is melodramatic, but the contrasts nonetheless do characterize his sensibility, because once his mind is focused on death there is no middle ground in which he can live. In *King Lear* these meditative antitheses are not only acted out by Lear himself but also inform every part of the play's action. For like Ecclesiastes, *King Lear* is composed of oppositions, oppositions between weeping and laughing, seeking and losing, being silent and speaking, loving and hating. The characters embody such contrasts: the spirituality of Cordelia is opposed to the concupiscence of Goneril and Regan, the piety of Edgar to the rapaciousness of Edmond, the selfless service of Kent to the self-serving of Oswald, the kindness of Albany to the sadism of Cornwall.

Some of these oppositions are combined in single characterizations, especially those of the Fool and Cordelia, but also those of Gloucester and Lear. The Fool's embodiment of the paradoxes of wisdom and folly that run through Ecclesiastes is of course obvious. He incarnates these paradoxes in his traditional role, in his dress, and in his speech; and he does so with the bias toward the broken heart that is characteristic both of Ecclesiastes and of the play. Enid Welsford remarks that "the Fool sees that when the match between the good and the evil is played by the intellect alone it must end in stalemate, but when the heart joins in the game then the decision is immediate and final. 'I will tarry, the Fool will stay—And let the wise man fly.' She adds that this "is the unambiguous wisdom of the madman who sees the truth," and that it "is decisive" because it reflects the way that normal human beings see the world feelingly.[5] I think that though this is perhaps true, the Fool's "whirling ambiguities" carry a burden that is further reminiscent of Ecclesiastes and less comforting. The Fool tells Lear that when Lear made his daughters his mothers,

> Then they for sudden joy did weep,
>   And I for sorrow sung,
> That such a king should play bo-peep,
>   And go the fools among.   (1.4.156–59)

Besides providing the keynote of his own characterization, this particular condensation of emotions is also eventually associated with the moment of death itself in the play. The paradoxical fusion of the extremities of joy and sorrow was often noted in the Renaissance commentaries on the passions,[6] but its identification with death is peculiar to *Lear*. The correspondence between the two is suggested in the old ballad that the Fool seems to be adapting:

> Some men for sodayne joye do wepe
>   And some in sorrow syng:
> When that they lie in daunger depe,
>   To put away mournyng.[7]

It is that shadow of mourning in the Fool, the association of the Fool with Death that is always incipient in his traditional role as the teller of the truths of human vanity and mortality, that makes it particularly appropriate for Lear to conflate him with

Cordelia at the end of the play, when he says, "And my poor fool is hanged" (5.3.281).

Cordelia's own combination of opposites is profound, but the play's most manifest combinations of the extremes that are traced in Ecclesiastes occur in the actions as well as characterizations of Lear and Gloucester, the two aged and dying protagonists who participate in, and must acknowledge the being of, all of their children, the loving and the hateful, the legitimate and the illegitimate. Indeed a large part of the action of the play consists of Lear's and Gloucester's oscillation between extremes that are never ameliorated, that tear at them, and that ultimately kill them.

Gloucester's initial arrogance in his talk of Edmond's bastardry yields very quickly to the demoralizing thought that his legitimate son seeks his death; and the "good sport" (1.1.22) of the scene of Edmond's conception is eventually contrasted with the malignant horror of the scene in which Gloucester is blinded. Edgar, who makes the latter contrast explicit, also tries to treat it homiletically: "The dark and vicious place where thee he got / Cost him his eyes" (5.3.163–64); but the symmetry of Edgar's formulation does not efface our own sense of the gross disparity between the two scenes. And the same is true of Gloucester's states of mind on the heath, after his blinding. Edgar's sententious efforts to preserve his father from despair finally only intensify our sense of the alternations between despair and patience that punctuate Gloucester's feelings, alternations that continue to the point of his death, and that actually constitute it. Near the end Gloucester, in his anguish, says to Edgar that "a man may rot even here" (5.2.8). Edgar's famous response—

Men must endure
Their going hence even as their coming hither.
Ripeness is all.   (5.2.9–11)

—might well be a verse in Ecclesiastes. (The exhausted tone of Ecclesiastes is generally apposite to the Gloucester plot.) "Ripeness" is a metaphor not for the fullness of life, but for the need to be resigned to the arbitrariness of its ending. As the context itself suggests, Edgar is evoking a traditional image of ripe fruit dropping from a tree and then rotting.[8] "Ripeness is all" is Gloucester's epitaph.

Similar stark contrasts of feeling, on a far more massive scale, inform Lear's movement toward death, and in his case there is not even the patina of moral commentary. The Fool's comments, which are the analogues of Edgar's, are almost always morally equivocal, and they are entirely absorbed with the paradoxical oppositions that compose Lear's condition. In the second childhood of age, Lear is at the same time "every inch a king" (4.5.107), and though he sometimes enacts these roles simultaneously, he cannot mediate between them: they remain in opposition until the play's end. His sense of humility grows, but it alternates with his wrath, it never replaces it. He howls at his last appearance in the play, as he did at his first. His increasing apprehension, early in the play, of the wrong he did Cordelia is balanced by his excoriations of his other daughters and by the fury of his madness, just as later in the play the joy of his recovery of Cordelia is balanced by the desolation of his loss of her. He imagines kneeling and humbling himself as a child before Cordelia in prison, but he presumes at the same time to be one of "God's spies," taking upon himself "the mystery of things" (5.3.16–17).[9] And the yoking of such disparities continues until his death, and in the very moment of it. His very last words express the hope— or delusion—that Cordelia is alive. They join with, they do not transform, the knowledge that she will never return.

The schematized world of *King Lear* has encouraged many critics to compare it to the morality plays, which are similarly composed of radically opposing states of feeling and being—virtue and vice, despair and hope, good and evil, angels and devils, and which, as in all the major tragedies, provide a resource for Shakespeare's representation of the dynamics of passion in the hero. But *Lear* clearly does not have the spiritual resolution of the moralities. In the moralities the summons of death is not ultimately an end but a beginning that retrospectively gives meaning to the large contrasts of human existence. In *King Lear*, on the other hand, as in Ecclesiastes, the summons is to an absolute ending whose allegorical retrospect of existence is not morally comprehensible. Edgar tries to make it so for his father's death, and there is perhaps a rough, if barbaric moral economy in Gloucester's destruction by his bastard son; but the Gloucester plot, in any case, is only the secondary plot of *King Lear*. The primary plot is Lear's, and even Edgar cannot moralize his story. He says of the spectacle of Lear's meeting with Gloucester on the heath, "I would not take this from report; it is, / And my heart breaks at it" (4.5.137–38). The verb *is* in Edgar's comment suggests that Lear's suffering presents us with the world of unmediated existential extremes we find in Ecclesiastes, where "as *is* the good, so *is* the sinner." The growth in Lear's understanding itself suggests this world. Lear does change on the heath. His own suffering allows him to feel, almost literally to touch, the pain of poor Tom and of the Fool and of poor naked wretches everywhere. This compassion is important and deeply moving. The sympathetic experience of pain establishes a human community in a play that seems otherwise to represent its Apocalyptic dissolution, and it informs our sense of Lear's heroic stature. But his compassion should also not be romanticized, for the knowledge of human frailty that his suffering brings him increases his sorrow to the point of madness. Critics sometimes talk of the "privilege" of Lear's madness, but if we consult our own experience of mentally infirm human beings, we will, like Edgar, know better. It is a horror, and an anticipation of "the promis'd end / Or image of that horror" (5.3.238–39) that we witness in Cordelia's death.[10]

Cordelia's death is, characteristically, preceded by her reunion with Lear after he awakens from his madness, a scene that has frequently been treated as if it were the climax of the action and that has often been compared with the reunion of Pericles and Marina in Shakespeare's later romance. The two scenes have many elements in common: both show old and exhausted fathers, decomposed by suffering, reunited with daughters from whom they have long been separated and who seem to bring them back to life. In both the recognitions are luminous; and both have verse of extraordinary lyric intensity. But the two scenes are also profoundly different in their immediate and eventual effects as well as in their generic contexts. Pericles' recovery of Marina is at once a recovery of his identity and an acknowledgment of its definition in the stream of time. For though, "wild in [his] beholding" (scene 21: 208), he draws Marina to himself and embraces her, he also immediately dreams of his eventual reunion with his wife and anticipates giving Marina away in marriage. He in addition hears the music of the spheres, a music that helps give Marina's nurture of him the sense of the comic intelligibility, if not miracle, of rebirth: "O, come hither," he tells her, "Thou that begett'st him that did thee beget" (scene 21: 182–83). The scene invokes the combination of joy and pain that is habitual in *King Lear*, but with a diametrically different accent. As Pericles recognizes Marina, he says:

> O Helicanus, strike me, honoured sir,
> Give me a gash, put me to present pain,
> Lest this great sea of joys rushing upon me
> O'erbear the shores of my mortality,
> And drown me with their sweetness!   (scene 21: 178–82)

Pericles' mixture of joy and pain is a guarantee of renewed life rather than an expression of its ending; and he later discriminates the pattern of the fortunate fall in all his suffering, suffering that is the prelude to joy and that heightens it: "you gods. Your present kindness / Makes my past miseries sports" (scene 22: 62–63).

The pattern, as well as the texture, of Lear's experience is the reverse. Lear tells Kent at the outset of the play that he had "thought to set [his] rest / On [Coredelia's] kind nursery" (1.1.123–24), and it is the peculiar nursing, rather than rebirth, of Lear that we witness in the bedside scene in which, attended by a doctor, he is reunited with Cordelia. For Cordelia ministers not only to an aged father but also to a man transformed by age into a child again. The metaphor of age as second childhood pervades the sources of *King Lear*, and Shakespeare himself tends to give it a harsh, if not grotesque, inflection in the play.[11] The Fool speaks of the King putting down his breeches and making his daughters his mothers (1.4.153–55), and in the scene in which Lear awakens from his madness, the metaphor is disturb-

ingly acted out. Lear kneels to Cordelia when he recognizes her
and says,

> I am a very foolish, fond old man,
> Fourscore and upward,
> Not an hour more nor less; and to deal plainly,
> I fear I am not in my perfect mind.   (4.6.53–56)

As Barbara Everett points out, that Lear should have to kneel
and confess the infirmity of age to his evil daughters is "terrible,"
but that he should do so to Cordelia as well "has also something
of the terrible in it." [12] The Fool repeatedly rebukes Lear for giving away his power and turning his family relationships upside
down, and Lear's behavior in the opening scene would seem to
justify those rebukes. But there is a sad irony in the Fool's
speeches, for as Montaigne suggested and as the play itself eventually shows, human beings of "fourscore and upward" usually
cannot do otherwise. [13] We often have no choice but to become
the parents of our parents in their old age and to treat them as
children; and it is painful because whether our motives verge
toward Cordelia's or toward Goneril and Regan's (and they may
do both) the nursing of parents is not nourishment for future
life but the preparation for death. It is directly so for Lear. The
music he hears in his reunion with Cordelia suggests no larger
life into which he can be incorporated, and his recovery of her is
the immediate prelude to his excruciating loss of her as well as
to his own death. In the manner of the whole play, it is a joy that
heightens sorrow, that makes it heartbreaking.

Dr. Johnson found Cordelia's death unendurable, if not be-
wildering, and he wished to avoid it. He protested that "Shakespeare has suffered the virtue of Cordelia to perish in a just
cause, contrary to the natural ideas of justice, to the hope of the
reader, and, what is yet more strange, to the faith of the chronicles." He added, "I was many years ago so shocked by Cordelia's
death, that I know not whether I ever endured to read again the
last scenes of the play till I undertook to revise them as an edi-
tor." [14] Adaptations of *King Lear*, notably Nahum Tate's, which left
Cordelia and Lear alive and united at the end of the play, in fact

held the English stage for over a century and a half,[15] and there is, as Johnson's commentary suggests, an inner logic to them, for they are really re-revisions of the Lear story and inherent within it. All of Shakespeare's own sources—the old play of *King Leir*, Holinshed, Spenser, and others—end (in the short term, at least) by giving life and victory to Cordelia and Lear.[16] Only Shakespeare does not, and his insistence on Cordelia's death and Lear's final agony is too deliberate to be denied. Lear and Cordelia's union in death is at the heart of Shakespeare's rendition of the Lear story. It is prepared for by every scene in which they appear together, including their earlier reunion, and it is the event that not only concludes the tragedy, but wholly informs it. We cannot deny it, however much we wish to and however much the play itself makes us with to.

A modern understanding of the psychology of dying can help illuminate this phenomenon.[17] Freud's discussion of *King Lear* in his essay "The Theme of the Three Caskets" is especially pertinent. He argues that the choice among the three daughters with which *King Lear* begins is the choice of death. Cordelia, in her muteness, he says, is the representation of death and, as in the depiction of such choices in the myths and fairy tales that *King Lear* resembles, her portrayal as the most beautiful and desirable of the three women expresses the inherent, often unconscious, human wish to deny death. "Lear is not only an old man: he is a dying man," and this reality subsumes both "the extraordinary premiss of the division of his inheritance" in the opening scene and the overpowering effect of the final scene: "Lear carries Cordelia's dead body on to the stage. Cordelia is Death. If we reverse the situation it becomes intelligible and familiar to us. She is the Death-goddess who, like the Valkyrie in German mythology, carries away the dead hero from the battlefield. Eternal wisdom, clothed in primaeval myth, bids the old man renounce love, choose death and make friends with the necessity of dying."[18]

Freud's identification of Cordelia with Lear's death suggests the kind of allegorization that often exasperates literary critics, but in this instance, at least, it seems just. Shakespeare's characterization of Cordelia is very luminous, but it is also very sharply focussed. She is from first to last a function of Lear's character, a part of him to which we know he must return. She is clearly the person who counts most to him, and in the extraordinary crowded action of the play it is his relation to her that we most attend to and that most organizes our responses. Their relationship is the emotional as well as structural spine of the play. Cordelia is the absolute focus of Lear's attention, and ours, in the opening scene; it is Lear's rejection of her that initiates the tragic action; and during that ensuing, often diffuse, action neither he nor we can ever forget her. The Fool, who is Cordelia's surrogate, does not allow us to, both because he keeps her constantly in Lear's mind on the heath and because the combination of love and sorrow that he brings to Lear prepares us for a similar combination in Cordelia's final role. The collocation of her reunion with Lear and his loss of her is of a piece with all the words of the Fool that weep for joy and sing for sorrow, and it constitutes the same paradox of heartbreak and death.

The association of Cordelia and death, which Lear himself momentarily suggests in the opening scene of the play, when he says, "So be my grave my peace as here I give / Her father's heart from her," is apparent in the scene's literal action as well. Freud contends that Cordelia's silence directly connotes death, as muteness often does in dreams.[19] But Cordelia also speaks in the scene, and what she says indicates clearly enough that Lear's rejection of her is precisely his denial of the impending death that he ostensibly acknowledges in the very act of dividing his kingdom and in his explicit announcement that he wishes "to shake all cares and business from our age," and "Unburdened crawl toward death" (1.1.39, 41). Cordelia tells her father that she loves him "According to [her] bond, no more nor less." She goes on to say:

> Good my lord,
> You have begot me, bred me, loved me.
> I return those duties back as are right fit—
> Obey you, love you, and most honour you.
> Why have my sisters husbands if they say
> They love you all? Haply, when I shall wed

That lord whose hand must take my plight shall carry
Half my love with him, half my care and duty.
Sure, I shall never marry like my sisters.   (1.1.93, 95–103)

Cordelia exhibits not a little of her father's own stubbornness in this speech, but though that trait may explain the manner of her speech, it does not account for what, as Kent remarks, she "justly think'st, and hast most rightly said." (1.1.183). What she declares quite clearly in these lines is not only that she must have the freedom to love a husband, but also that it is in the nature of things for parents to be succeeded by children and for her to have a future that Lear cannot absorb or control. Her peculiar gravity in this scene, the spareness and sternness of her insistence on the word *bond* as well as her reiteration of the word *nothing*, reflects more than her temperament. It also suggests, even this early in the play, the particular sense of the nature of things that is evoked in Ecclesiastes—the sense of human vanity that comes with the awareness of the ultimate bond with death. At any rate, it is to the natural realities given expression in Cordelia's speech that Lear responds. His rage against her, like his cosmological rage throughout the play, is his refusal to go "gentle into that good night," his heroic, as well as unavailing, attempt to deny death and hold on to life.

Shakespeare's depiction of this rage and denial is intelligible in Renaissance as well as modern terms. Montaigne's discussion of death and dying in "Of Judging of Others Death," for example, is even more apposite to Lear than it is to Macbeth. In support of his contention that "no one of us thinkes it sufficient to be but one," Montaigne remarks, in an argument that has analogies with Freud's, that a dying man "will hardly beleeve he is come to [the] point" of death, and that "no wher doth hopes deceit ammuse us more." "The reason is," he says, "that we make too much account of our selves. It seemeth, that the generality of things doth in some sort suffer for our annullation, and takes compassion of our state." "We entertaine and carry all with us," Montaigne continues, whence it followeth, that we deeme our death to be some great matter, and which passeth not so easily, nor without a solemne consultation of the Starres; *Tot circa unum caput tumultuantes Deos. So many Gods keeping a stirre about one mans life.* And so much the more we thinke it, by how much the more we praise our selves. What? should so much learning and knowledge be lost with so great dammage, without the Destinies particular care? A soule so rare and exemplar, costs it no more to be killed, then a popular and unprofitable soule? This life, that covereth so many others, of whom so many other lives depend, that, for his use possesseth so great a part of the world and filleth so many places, is it displaced as that which holdeth by its owne simple string?[20]

Shakespeare's depiction of Lear is clearly informed by such ideas. His portrait is far more sympathetic than Montaigne's, but the ironies remain similar, even though Lear himself becomes partly aware of them. Lear can and does become humbled, but rage and cosmological pretension nonetheless characterize him throughout the play. His rage reaches its apogee during the time when his denial of what Cordelia stands for is literalized by her absence from the play. Her return in act 4 heralds his significant recognition that he is "but one"—"They told me I was everything; 'tis a lie, I am not ague-proof" (4.5.104–5)—and permits him to recover from his madness when he is physically reunited with her. But his inescapable attachment to her, his bond with her, is always a prefiguration of his death. It is often difficult in our experience of *King Lear* to understand that Lear's denial of death is represented as much in his love for Cordelia as in his rage against her. It is even more difficult, but crucial, to understand that Cordelia's own love is itself a function of this denial, that the expression of her love at the end of the play is as much a signification of Lear's death as is the muteness of that love at the start. Granville Barker hints at such a meaning as well as at Cordelia's general symbolic properties in his comments on her characterization. He observes that she does not change in the play, and that her cry of "No cause, no cause" to Lear at their reunion is essentially of a piece with her earlier declaration of "Nothing, my lord." He remarks that though "it is no effort to her to love her father better than herself, . . . this supremest virtue, as we count it, is no gain to him," and he asks, "Is there, then, an impotence in such goodness, lovely as we find it? And is this why Shakespeare lets her slip out of the play . . . to her death, as if, for all her beauty of spirit, she were not of so much account?"[21] The questions Granville Barker asks and the paradox he discriminates are central to Cordelia's characterization and are at the center of most of the play's other paradoxes as well. They are best explained, I think, in terms (which Granville Barker himself does not use) of the phenomenon of the denial of death, what Montaigne calls "hopes deceit."[22]

In all the myths of the choice among three sisters that Freud finds analogous to *King Lear* (and he includes the choice among the three caskets in *The Merchant of Venice*), the woman representing the power of death is transformed into a woman representing the power of love. Contradictions and contraries of this kind— when one thing is replaced by its precise opposite—are characteristic of the process of condensation in dreams; but Freud relates such contradictions in *King Lear* primarily to the human disposition to deny what cannot be tolerated and to make use of the imagination "to satisfy the wishes that reality does not satisfy." The profound human wish to deny "the immutable law of death" is represented both in the identification of the most beautiful sister with death and in the presence of choice itself: "Choice stands in the place of necessity, of destiny. In this way man overcomes death, which he has recognized intellectually. No greater triumph of wish-fulfilment is conceivable. A choice is made where in reality there is obedience to a compulsion; and what is chosen is not a figure of terror, but the fairest and most desirable of women."[23]

In the old play of *King Leir* the King has an explicit political motive that is associated with his testing of his daughter's love as well as with the division of the kingdom, and the two wicked daughters are forewarned of it while the good one is not. All three daughters, moreover, are unmarried, and the issue of their marriages is related to the love test and to politics. Shakespeare almost entirely shears away such surface motives and rationalizations for Lear's action in order to make its underlying motive of denial more stark and more compelling.[24] The whole scene echoes with negations and contradictions. Its sense of high order and ceremony is prefaced by Gloucester's casual talk of ungoverned instinct. The ceremony itself is a decoronation, deeply reminiscent of Richard II's undecking of "the pompous body of a king" as well as of Richard's ambivalence: "Ay, no; no, ay; for I must nothing be" (*Richard II*, 4.1.240, 191). The pun is not only on "Ay" for "I," but also "no" for "know." Richard knows no "I" and sees that he is to be no "I."[25] He thus seems to indicate and accept, more clearly than Lear ever does, that the loss of his crown also constitutes the loss of his life, that "nothing" is death. This meaning of the word becomes unmistakeably plain in his final speech in prison when he says, "Thus play I in one person many people,"

> But whate'er I be,
> Nor I, nor any man that but man is,
> With nothing shall be pleased till he be eased
> With being nothing.   (5.5.31, 38–41)

Lear himself does not acknowledge the ambivalence which Richard exhibits in resigning the throne, but he unquestionably acts it out. He invests Cornwall and Albany with his "power / Preeminence, and all the large effects / That troop with majesty," but he wishes at the same time to "retain / The name and all th'addition to a king." (1.1.130–32, 135–36) Richard II also cleaves, unavailingly, to the "king's name," and in his case the implications of that wish are explicitly related to the Renaissance concept of the mystical union between the king's two bodies, between the body natural that is subject to time and death, and the body politic that is divine and immortal.[26] Richard's repeated invocations of his name ("Arm, arm, my name!" [3.2.82]) signify the imminent severing of this union and his growing consciousness of death. Even though the universe of *King Lear* is not Christian, Lear's wish to "retain / The name and all th'addition to a king" would probably have been understood in the same context of ideas and have suggested the same implicit focus upon mortality. But in any case, his wish, even on its face, contradicts his ostensible desire to resign the "sway," "revenue" and "execution" of the king's power (1.1.136–37), and that contradiction governs his manner, his speech, and his actions throughout the opening scene.

The contraries that compose Cordelia in the scene are less obvious but more profound and more moving. What is compelling about her from the outset is that she continuously represents both sides of the process of denial: the heart's sorrow as well as its joy. She represents the vanity of denial but also its animating power, the love of life as well as the inescapability of death, the mother that nurtures us, as Freud suggests, as well as the Mother Earth that finally receives us.[27] She tells Lear the truth of his dying in the opening scene: "Nothing, my lord." She stands in mute rebuke to the folly of his attempt to deny it. And she eventually becomes that truth when she lies lifeless in his arms. But at the same time the very telling of that truth is replete with love—"What shall Cordelia speak? Love and be silent" (1.1.62)—which is what makes Lear's rejection of her seem unnatural on the literal as well as symbolic level. As the play progresses she comes more and more to represent everything that binds Lear most nobly to life and that makes his protest against death at once heartbreaking and heroic. Freud speaks of the resistance to death as essentially a reflex of the ego's wish to be immortal. But Freud undervalues human love, for another reason that we do not wish to die and see those close to us die, even the very old, is that we are capable of cherishing and loving others. Cordelia is an incarnation of this capacity.

Cordelia's representation of such love in *King Lear* is given religious, and specifically Christian overtones, and perhaps the greatest pain of her death, and of her tragic embodiment of the futility of the denial of death, is that the promise of these overtones also proves empty. Cordelia's counterpart in the old chronicle play of *King Leir* is, like the whole of the play, explicitly homiletic and Christian. When she is rejected by her father, she turns to "him which doth protect the just, / In him will poore

Cordella put her trust," and later, as she acknowledges her sisters' "blame," she prays for God's forgiveness both of them and her father:

> Yet God forgive both him, and you and me,
> Even as I doe in perfit charity.
> I will to Church, and pray unto my Saviour,
> That ere I dye, I may obtayne his favour. (331–32, 1090–93)[28]

Cordella's trust in God is fully vindicated at the end of the play when she and Leir are triumphantly reunited and he is restored to love and dignity.

Shakespeare deliberately intensifies, at the same time that he transmutes, the old play's association of Cordella with Christianity. There are unmistakable New Testament echoes in *King Lear*, and most of them cluster around Cordelia. They begin in the opening scene, when France uses the language of miracle and faith to question Lear's judgment of Cordelia (1.1.220–22) and when he takes her as his wife:

> Fairest Cordelia, that art most rich, being poor;
> Most choice, forsaken; and most loved, despised:
> Thee and thy virtues here I seize upon. (1.1.250–52)

The allusion to 2 *Corinthians* 6:10 is clear—"as poore, and yet [making] manie riche: as having nothing, and *yet* possessing all things"—and it resonates with the deepest preoccupations of the whole scene. The allusions and associations intensify at the end of the play. When Cordelia returns from France she says, "O dear father, / It is thy business that I go about" (4.3.23–24; cf. Luke 2:49); and shortly afterwards, the Gentleman who is sent to rescue Lear says,

> Thou hast a daughter
> Who redeems nature from the general curse
> Which twain have brought her to. (4.5.201–3)

] 123 [

At the very end Cordelia's death is associated with the Last Judgment (5.3.238–39), and Lear himself wishes for her revival in language that seems to echo the deepest of Christian beliefs:

> This feather stirs. She lives. If it be so,
> It is a chance which does redeem all sorrows
> That ever I have felt.   (5.3.240–42)

But she does not live, and Lear, whether he dies thinking she does or not, is not redeemed by her. For in the pagan world of *King Lear* the New Testament's conception of death, and life, is the denial; the reality is that of Ecclesiastes, the pilgrimage of the heart in the Old Testament that insists above all else that death cannot be denied. Shakespeare, in all the plots of *King Lear*, at once summons up and denies the most profound energies of the comic and romantic impulses of the chronicle play of *Leir*, as well as of his other sources.[29] We expect and wish, for example, for Gloucester to recognize his good son, Edgar, but he does so only at the very moment of his death and offstage, and we wish, as Kent does, that Lear will recognize him as his faithful servant Caius, and he never does. The most painful of these denials of our romantic expectations, however, is the treatment of Cordelia. By associating her role with the Christian hope of redemption,[30] as Dr. Johnson perceived, Shakespeare deliberately violates not only "the faith of the chronicles" but also the profoundest "hope of the reader." We ourselves are thus compelled not just to view the process of denial, but to undergo it and endure it. There is no deeper a generic transformation of a source in the canon, and it is the wellspring of the sense of grotesqueness as well as of desolation that is so peculiar to this tragedy.[31]

Such an understanding of the use to which Shakespeare puts Christian evocations in the pagan world of *King Lear* helps explain the luminous presence in the play of the kind of spirituality, in Lear no less than in Cordelia (as well as in the Fool and Kent), that no pagan author could have portrayed. It can also help clarify the religious issues that continue to vex criticism of the play. But it should not be interpreted to suggest that *King Lear* is a homily on the inadequacy of pagan virtue or that the play's conception of death is unique among Shakespeare's tragedies.[32] The sense that death defines human life and that after it, in Hamlet's last words, "the rest is silence" (5.2.310) is as germane to *Hamlet*, *Othello*, and *Macbeth*, which have manifest Christian settings, as it is to *King Lear*. Christian belief does give a providential perspective to death in those plays, most strongly in *Hamlet*, where the intimations of another world of being become a part of the hero's thought, and there is perhaps a sense that Lear, too, as he dies, perceives such a world. Bradley claimed that "though Lear is killed by an agony of pain, the agony in which he actually dies is one not of pain but of ecstasy," since Lear "is sure, at the last," that Cordelia lives. Bradley concluded that "to us perhaps, the knowledge that he is deceived may bring a culmination of pain: but, if it brings *only* that, I believe we are false to Shakespeare, and it seems almost beyond question that any actor is false to the text who does not attempt to express, in Lear's last accents and gestures and look, an unbearable *joy*."[33] A recent critic, basically agreeing with Bradley, adds that Lear's final words and gesture, "Look there, look there," refer to Cordelia's spirit, not her lips or physical life, and that they thus suggest a vision of eternal life.[34] But in *King Lear*, unlike *Pericles*, unbearable joy, the ecstasy of pain and sorrow, consistently means heartbreak and death, not life. It seems to me that Dr. Johnson, in his inability to accept Cordelia's death (and Bradley himself, in his judgment that her death is, for us as well as Lear, "a culmination of pain"), is closer to the truth. As Northrop Frye remarks,

> *King Lear* has been called a purgatorial tragedy, and if that means a structure even remotely like Dante's *Purgatorio*, we should expect to see, as we see in Dante, existence being taken over and shaped by a moral force. Our understanding of the tragedy, then, would have that qualified response in it that is inseparable from a moral or conceptual outlook. It is true that Lear has suffered terribly, but he has thereby gained, etc. Suffering is inevitable in the nature of things, yet, etc. But, of course, Lear is not saying anything like this at the end of the

play: what he is saying is that Cordelia is gone, and will never, never come back to him. Perhaps he thinks that she is coming back to life again, and dies of an unbearable joy. But we do not see this: all we see is an old man dying of an unbearable pain. The hideous wrench of agony which the death of Cordelia gives to the play is too much a part of the play even to be explained as inexplicable. And whatever else may be true, the vision of absurd anguish in which the play ends certainly is true.[35]

I think Frye is correct, whether one argues that Lear imagines Cordelia is coming back to life or that he imagines he sees her living spirit. A providential perspective in a tragedy, as opposed to a romance, which is what Bradley and others try to make *Lear* turn into, not only cannot fully explain the hero's actual suffering, but also cannot absorb it, whether that perspective is explicit, as it is in *Hamlet*, or inferred, as it may be in *King Lear*. Nor can it fundamentally mitigate the effect of that suffering on us. One can spend much time gauging the level of irony in the endings of the tragedies, but when we see or read these great plays we do not construe the endings, we feel them, and what we feel is a paramount sense of suffering and loss. The distinction of *King Lear* is that the death of Cordelia compounds that feeling and focuses it. All of us are pagan in our immediate response to dying and death. The final scene of *King Lear* is a representation—among the most moving in all drama—of the universality of this experience and of its immeasurable pain.

CHAPTER VI

SHAKESPEARE'S
HUMANISM

THE PREMISE OF THIS BOOK is that Shakespeare's plays represent enduring truths of our emotional and spiritual lives, that these truths help account for Shakespeare's enormous vitality in the classroom as well as the theater, and that they deserve our direct attention. These are not now fashionable assumptions. For over a decade, the reigning ideas in the criticism of Shakespeare and Renaissance literature, fostered largely but not exclusively by the schools of new historicism and cultural materialism, have been that literature as well as men and women are products of particular cultures and can only be understood in terms of them; that the very conception of the individual, who has a continuous and intelligible interior life, which can be understood from age to age, is a post-Enlightenment phenomenon; and that Elizabethan culture contested orthodox Christian ideas of providence and order and Shakespeare necessarily represented as well as reflected this contest. Thus, for example, the Marxist critic Jonathan Dollimore has argued that Jacobean as well as Shakespearian tragedy constitutes a rejection of Elizabethan orthodox ideology and a severance of "the connection between individuality and man, between subjectivity and the human condition." "Consequently," he argues, the tragedies deny "essentialist humanism," including "the 'tragic' belief in a human essence which by its own nature as well as its relation to the universal order of things, must inevitably suffer."[1] Stephen Greenblatt, the founder of new historicism, remarks that "the human subject itself" in the Renaissance was "remarkably unfree, the ideological product of the relations of power in a particular society." "Whenever I focused sharply," he writes, "upon a moment of apparently autonomous self-fashioning, I found not an epiphany of identity freely chosen but a cultural artifact."[2] The disposition of such critics has been to give enormous priority to Elizabethan culture, which was at first mostly construed as politics, but has more recently spread to a variety of sociological topics that Greenblatt has called "cultural negotiations."[3]

These notions can be, and increasingly have been, disputed on theoretical grounds,[4] but they are novel as well as extreme, and it is also important simply to remember older, and more abiding, tenets of literary criticism—and of life—that seem more reasonable and wise. To begin with, we should take seriously Sidney's distinction in the *Defence of Poesie* between the "right poet" and the historian and the philosopher. Whatever the ambiguities of Sidney's reasoning in differentiating the poet may be (his precise view of mimesis, for example),[5] it is clear enough that he agrees with the classical understanding that the poet unites the general and the particular in a way that historians and philosophers do not, and that the "Zodiack" of the poet's "owne wit" differs in kind from the powers of mind that are brought to bear on the writing of history and philosophy.[6]

A. D. Nuttall has suggested that such a difference governs how we respond to literature. He argues that literature presents an "experiential hypothesis" that is analogous to the concreteness of experience itself: "The fiction evokes from us, as we entertain the hypothesis, all the human energies and powers, the incipient commitments and defences which occur in experiential knowing, but are absent from cool, conceptual knowing."[7] Sidney himself makes much the same point when he says that the poet creates a "perfect picture" that "yeeldeth to the powers of the minde an image of that whereof the Philosopher bestoweth but a woordish description: which dooth neyther strike, pierce, nor possesse the sight of the soule so much as the other dooth."[8] The distinction deserves particular emphasis because the natural

bias toward historical or theoretical, if not philosophical, interests in most academic discourse has recently tended to engorge
literary criticism, not only in new historicist and cultural mate-
rialist writings but in their sources in structuralism and decon-
struction. A major criticism of the old "ideas-of-the-times"
historicism was not only that it homogenized the period (and
the author) but also that in treating Shakespeare's plays as documents or arguments it obliterated their individual and peculiar
dramatic life, and both charges remain true of the new fashion
as well.[9] Shakespeare, who Dryden said had "the largest and most
comprehensive soul," obviously responded to the heterodoxies
as well as orthodoxies of his time, and they are both reflected in
his work, but there is no evidence that he was nearly as interested in writing *about* them, or the contest between them, as his
critics are. He seems, on the contrary, to have been most interested in creating the kind of experience described in Dekker's
prologue to *If It Be Not Good* (1612), which praises the playwright
who can move the hearts of his audience, who can make even
the ignorant among them "applaud what their charm'd soul
scarce understands," "infus[ing] them" "With Raptures, Into a
second." He says that such a playwright

> Can give an Actor, Sorrow, Rage, Joy, Passion,
> Whilst hee againe (by selfe same Agitation)
>> Commands the Hearers, sometimes drawing out *Teares*,
>> Then Smiles and fills them both with Hopes &
>> Feares.[10]

A critic, of course, has the right to treat Shakespeare's plays as
political or sociological documents and to "foreground" their
spoken or unspoken ideological premises, but the reader has the
equal right to distrust his criticism if it displaces the real foreground of the plays and ignores or deforms the kinds of passions
and responses to them that Dekker is talking about and that
Shakespeare's plays themselves have managed to create for audiences for four centuries. Readers and audiences also have the
right to remain less interested in what reduces Shakespeare's

work to the discourse of any of his contemporaries than in what makes each of his plays so alive and different.

In his homage to Shakespeare in the first folio, Ben Jonson writes that Shakespeare is the "Soul of the age! / The applause, delight! the wonder of our stage," but he says also that his greatness would have been proclaimed by ancient playwrights as well, because "He was not of an age, but for all time!" The tribute to Shakespeare as the soul of his age is less well known than the praise of him as timeless, but apparently in Jonson's judgment— and he was a classicist as well as a practicing dramatist—the two were not incompatible. There is the suggestion, instead, that they are connected, that the fidelity of Shakespeare's representations of the soul of his own age is at least part of what enables his plays to live beyond that age. Jonson's praise is directed to Shakespeare's language and the way he delights an audience, but the point seems equally valid for an understanding of what the plays imitate. Macbeth's quest, for example, may reflect Elizabethan "capitalist" individualism,[11] but that reflection in turn expresses Shakespeare's deeper interest in the emotional and spiritual roots of the quest for absolute self-sufficiency that exist in all men and that Augustine had discriminated over a thousand years earlier. Similarly, much in *King Lear* may constitute a protest against social injustice and corruption, Elizabethan or otherwise,[12] but these very protests are at the same time, and more formidably, images of the deeper and abiding rage against the conditions of human mortality, the immanence of death in human life as well as the inescapable fact of it. Finally, though Othello's tragedy can be construed as a protest against Elizabethan religious orthodoxy and patriarchal sexual politics,[13] these protests have tragic interest because they dramatize inescapable erotic discontents in any civilized society.

A century and a half after Ben Jonson, Dr. Johnson wrote, in his own tribute to Shakespeare, "Nothing can please many, and please long, but just representations of general nature. Particular manners can be known to few, and therefore few only can judge how nearly they are copied. The irregular combinations of fanciful invention may delight a-while, by that novelty of which the common satiety of life sends us all in quest; but the pleasures of

sudden wonder are soon exhausted, and the mind can only repose on the stability of truth." He went on to say, in words that
echo those of Hamlet's injunction to the players:

> Shakespeare is above all writers, at least above all mod-
> ern writers, the poet of nature; the poet that holds up to
> his readers a faithful mirrour of manners and of life. His
> characters are not modified by the customs of particular
> places, unpractised by the rest of the world; by the pe-
> culiarities of studies or professions, which can operate
> but upon small numbers; or by the accidents of transient
> fashions or temporary opinions: they are the genuine
> progeny of common humanity, such as the world will
> always supply, and observation will always find. His per-
> sons act and speak by the influence of those general pas-
> sions and principles by which all minds are agitated, and
> the whole system of life is continued in motion. In the
> writings of other poets a character is too often an indi-
> vidual; in those of Shakespeare it is commonly a spe-
> cies.[14]

Johnson's assertion of the universal is less categorical than it
may seem—he is really arguing for Shakespeare's capacity to apprehend the species in the individual[15]—but he still overdoes it.
Shakespeare's characters are clearly modified by the custom of
particular places. All of Shakespeare's tragic heroes exist in a specific political and cultural context, and in the Roman plays that
context is emphatic, if not primary. Coriolanus, for example, is
not fully intelligible unless he is understood, as Shakespeare
seems to have wished him to be understood, as a product of a
particular Roman culture, what Nuttall has called a shame culture,[16] and it can be misleading to psychoanalyze his vulnerability to shame without considering that Shakespeare presents it in
the context not only of Coriolanus's particular society but of
that society's heroic ideals. On the other hand, we can recognize
and understand these very elements of shame because they are
part of our own psychological histories. Nuttall finds them in the
culture of English public schools, but they are a recognizable and

continuing feature of all adolescence and of the remains as well as memory of adolescence in adults. "Dennis and Rhymer," Johnson writes, "think [Shakespeare's] Romans not sufficiently Roman. . . . Dennis is offended, that Menenius, a senator of Rome, should play the buffoon." Johnson answers that Shakespeare "knew that Rome, like every other society, had men of all dispositions; and wanting a buffoon, he went into the senate-house for that which the senate-house would certainly have afforded him." [17] This remark is celebrated not only because it is elegantly stated but because it is so obviously true.

Johnson's claim essentially echoes Aristotle's in the *Poetics*. "Poetry," Aristotle writes, "tends rather to express what is universal, whereas History relates to particular events as such. By an exhibition of what is universal or typical is meant the representation of what a certain type of person is likely or is bound to say or do in a given situation. This is the aim of the Poet, though at the same time he attaches the names of specific persons to the types." [18] Aristotle, like Johnson (and Sidney and Hamlet), assumes that there are universal, if not "essential," characteristics of human behavior, and that it is the purpose and distinction of the poet to imitate them. It is unlikely that he and most other writers in the last two millennia are wrong and a coterie of academic critics of the last decade right.

Most Western writers have also assumed that whatever its cultural contingencies, the individual exists and can be defined as a being with a reasonably continuous and particular identity, a particular configuration of body and soul, emotions and thought, habits and patterns of choice and action. One would not have imagined that at least an approximation of such notions of the individual (implicit or explicit, more emphatic or less) in the Renaissance or at any other period would need justification, but in the Emperor's New Clothes court of many recent critics, it apparently does. For these critics argue, in effect, that culture (by which they usually mean politics) is everything. They claim that the borders defining an individual are infinitely permeable, and that the very notion of an individual upon which Freud and modern psychology depend is anachronistic, that the idea of the individual did not yet exist in the Renaissance. Ste-

phen Greenblatt, for example, claims that in the proceedings of
the court that tried to establish whether the man claiming to be
Martin Guerre was an impostor, any ideas of an "irreducible
identity," "continuous selfhood" or, as in Freud, at least "the
dream of authentic possession," were "irrelevant to the point of
being unthinkable." He cites Montaigne's suspicion that the case
was not one that a judge could determine with luminous and
flawless clarity as evidence of his assertions ("A tuer les gens, il
faut une clarté lumineuse et nette").[19]

Cultural materialists like Jonathan Dollimore argue for a
more progressive change in conceptions of the self, the modern
concept being a consequence of the rise of capitalism, but he too
gives absolute authority to the social contingencies of individual
identity and enlists Montaigne in his cause. He cites Montaigne's
conclusion, in "Of Custom," that "the lawes of conscience, which
we say to proceed from nature, rise and proceed of custome," as
well as Montaigne's assertion in "An Apology of *Raymond Sebond*"
that "*there is no constant existence, neither of our being, nor of the objects*
[of experience]. And we, and our judgement, and all mortall
things else do uncessantly rowle, turne and passe away." He also
quotes Montaigne's claim that "we have no communication with
being; for every humane nature is ever in the middle between
being borne and dying; giving nothing of itselfe but an obscure
appearence and shadow, and an uncertaine and weake opinion.
And if perhaps you fix your thought to take its being; it would
be even, as if one should go about to grasp the water: for, how
much the more he shal close and presse that, which by its owne
nature is ever gliding, so much the more he shall loose what he
would hold and fasten."[20]

Greenblatt basically takes Montaigne out of context—the
essay, "Of the Lame or Cripple," from which he quotes is about
the imperfectability of human judgment in all matters, not about
the indeterminacy of identity; and the alleged radical heterodoxies Dollimore cites, in addition to being quite conventionally
Christian, are throughout the essays consistently celebrated by
Montaigne as a part of his understanding of himself: "My selfe,
who brag so curiously to embrace and particularly to allow the
commodities of life; whensoever I looke precisely into it finde

nothing therein but winde. But what? we are nothing but winde. And the very winde also, more wisely then we loveth to bluster and to be in agitation: And is pleased with his owne offices, without desiring stability or solidity; qualities that be not his owne."[21]

But aside from these particularities, Montaigne's *Essais* as a whole, as opposed to the individual statements that can be pillaged from them, stand, along with Shakespeare's plays, as perhaps the preeminent refutation of the notion that the Renaissance could not conceive of subjectivity. There can be nothing more clear than that Montaigne's entire enterprise is to explore his individual identity, his thoughts, his feelings, his habits both of mind and body, his body's relation to his mind, his way of thinking and understanding, his reading, his peculiar interests, his tics of behavior; and it is also palpably clear that however much a fiction the self he creates may be, it has mimetic truth, it is one that we can still individually and collectively understand—and learn from. I think that it would have confirmed Montaigne's view, in "Of Pedantisme," that learned men can "be distracted even from common sense,"[22] to have been informed that his friend Etienne de La Boétie did not have even a dream of an "authentic possession" of individual character, or to have been told that his own "manners," which he so frequently seeks to "compose," were inauthentic as well.[23]

"Others fashion man," Montaigne says in the opening of "Of Repenting,"

> I repeat him; and represent a particular one, but ill made; and whom were I to forme a new, he should be far other than he is; but he is now made. And though the lines of my picture change and vary, yet loose they not themselves.... I cannot settle my object; it goeth so unquietly and staggering, with a naturall drunkennesse. I take it in this plight, as it is at th'instant I ammuse my selfe about it. I describe not the essence, but the passage; not a passage from age to age, or as the people reckon, from seaven yeares to seaven, but from day to day, from minute to minute. My history must be fitted to the pres-

ent. I may soone change, not onely fortune, but intention. It is a counter-roule of divers and variable
accidents, and irresolute imaginations, and sometimes
contrary: whether it be that my selfe am other, or that I
apprehend subjects, by other circumstances and consid-
erations.[24]

Montaigne clearly considers mutability and change to be the virtual substance of his subject, but neither here nor elsewhere does
he therefore assume there is no subject. "I study my selfe," he
writes in "Of Experience," "more than any other subject. It is my
supernaturall Metaphisike, it is my naturall Philosophy."[25] He
also says that it is an identifiably particular subject: "There is no
man (if he listen to himselfe) that doth not discover in himselfe
a peculiar forme of his, a swaying forme, which wrestleth against
the institution, and against the tempests of passions, which are
contrary unto him."[26] Finally, however, he also assumes, and
states explicitly in a well-known sentence immediately following
his discussion of his changeableness in "Of Repenting," that
identity involves sameness as well as difference, that his subject
is representative as well as particular: *"Every man beareth the whole
stampe of humane condition."*[27]

In "Of Experience," in a secular revision of the traditional
Christian introspective search for the *imago Dei* common to all
men, Montaigne specifically argues that his introspection helps
him both relate to and understand others:

This long attention, I employ in considering my selfe,
enableth me also to judge indifferently [*passablement*—
passably] of others: And there are few things whereof I
speake more happily and excusably. It often fortuneth
me to see and distinguish more exactly the conditions of
my friends, than themselves do. I have astonied some by
the pertinency of mine own description, and have
warned him of himselfe. Because I have from mine infancy enured my selfe to view mine owne life in others
lives; I have thereby acquired a studious complexion
therein. And when I thinke on it, I suffer few things to

escape about me, that may in any sort fit the same;
whether countenances, humour or discourses. I stu-
diously consider all I am to eschew and all I ought to
follow. So by my friends productions I discover their inward inclinations.[28]

Montaigne's clear and deepest wish in his essays is to be self-
sufficient. "I care not so much what I am with others, as I respect
what I am in my selfe." He even writes that he wishes he did not
have a name, because it is not "sufficiently mine"[29] (the precise
predicament of Coriolanus). But Montaigne argues at the same
time that an individual is obliged to relate to others in order to
live:

Whatsoever it bee, either Art or nature, that imprints
this condition of life into us, by relation to others, it
doth us much more hurt then good. In going about to
frame appearances according to the common opinion,
wee defraud ourselves of our owne profits. Wee care not
so much, what our state, or how our being is in us, and
in effect, as wee doe how and what it is in the publike
knowledge of others. Even the goods of the minde, and
wisedome it selfe, seeme fruitlesse unto us, if onely enjoyed by us: except it be set forth to the open view and
approbation of others.[30]

Montaigne regrets this "condition of life," but he sees it, and
throughout his writing about himself, as well as others, he reck-
ons with it. As Jean Starobinski has remarked, Montaigne's
"inwardness" depends upon its communication with, and exter-
nalization, in the " 'outside' world, which Montaigne needs
equally to oppose and to observe." "The free mind," Starobinski
adds, "is not a solitary mind. It is opposed to the world and yet
it lives in the world. It is opposed to itself and yet it 'broods over
[its] thoughts.' Montaigne is undoubtedly one of those writers
most responsible for fleshing out our Western notion of individual existence. But he warns us to be on our guard: the individual

comes into possession of himself only through the image of himself reflected by others—all others."[31] Freud remarks analogously, if less elegantly, that the ego relates to objects "much as the body of an amoeba is related to the pseudopodia which it puts out," and he argues that this constant movement is necessary for the nourishment and very existence of the ego.[32]

I have quoted Montaigne at such length not only because his essays are a compelling assertion of the "humanism" that recent critics, who profess to draw upon him, have sought to discard, but also because he represents, in discursive form, many of the abiding human experiences that are to be found in Shakespearian drama. Shakespeare's temperament, I think, has more Platonic inclinations, it is modulated in the tragedies by a heroic vision Montaigne would have been unlikely to have shared, and it is in any case far less easy to discover than Montaigne's; but the affinities between the two are nonetheless considerable. Almost the same perceptions of human mortality and infirmity that tragically afflict Lear are discriminated, in a different key, throughout Montaigne's essays, but especially "An Apologie of Raymond Sebond," a work that can legitimately be considered one of the most significant sources of *King Lear*.[33] The perception in all four of the major tragedies of man's vanity and presumption in the face of death is an ironic undertow that is evident not only in Montaigne's explicit comments on the subject in "Of Judging of Others Death" but throughout the *Essais*. The sense in *All's Well That Ends Well* that "the web of our life is a mingled yarn, good and ill together," and that "our virtues would be proud if our faults whipped them not, and our crimes would despair if they were not cherished by our virtues" (4.3.74–77), which Shakespeare in that play seems to have drawn directly from Montaigne's "Upon Some Verses of Virgil," underlies all the plays and all of Montaigne.[34] The debate of Hector and Troilus over inherent and attributed value (2.2.8–192), which informs not only *Troilus and Cressida* but the protagonist's quest for heroic identity in the later Roman plays, is a profound preoccupation in Montaigne, not just in "Of Glorie," but in the very nature of the project of his *Essais*. Prospero's attempt to harmonize his passions and reason, which is epitomized in his speech on the rarer virtue of temperance that Shakespeare directly borrows from Montaigne,[35] and which is a counterpoint to the hero's suffering in all the tragedies, is part of Montaigne's very disposition and a central purpose of his essays.

These parallels, all of them deep, could easily be multiplied, but I want to touch on only one more, perhaps the most important, and that is the depiction of profound change in a human being, and particularly the portrayal of the actual process of change, of the intense movement of feelings and thoughts within him. The title of Starobinski's book on Montaigne, *Montaigne en mouvement* (*Montaigne in Motion*), is apposite. Montaigne actively represents as well as describes in his "day to day ... minute to minute" scrutiny of himself not only his constant changeableness but also the inner dynamics of change, the dynamics that are the consequence of the mixture within him of emotions and thoughts, of the pleasures and pains of his flesh and spirit, as well as of the opposition of his "peculiar forme" and passions to the contingencies of his society and environment. The depiction of these movements may be the greatest source of Montaigne's wisdom. It is certainly one of the greatest achievements of his essays.

It is also one of the greatest achievements of Shakespeare's plays, particularly the four major tragedies. In Montaigne's case, the representation of the actions of passion and thought and of the processes of change follows from the introspective yet public nature of his project in writing the *Essais* and from the consequent modulation of his Stoic disposition by the extraordinary honesty of his sensibility and the genius of his observation.[36] Shakespeare's genius, in addition, could draw upon the resources of drama. In particular, as I suggested at the outset of this book, by literalizing the schemata of the allegorical morality drama, by giving psychological and social dimension to its dynamics of moral choice, he could at once anatomize the inner life of his hero and depict its outward manifestations and causes, his relation to others and to the world. In Shakespeare's comedies and romances, where the heroes and heroines are progressively defined and dilated within a community, there is at least an equilibrium between the individual and communal definition of the self, and usually a movement from the former to the latter. In the tragedies, where the protagonist moves toward death, the one inescapably solitary human experience, and where his consciousness is progressively alienated from the community's, often to the point of what could be called psychotic awareness, the hero is increasingly isolated and the essential movement is inward. In the four major tragedies particularly, the result is a representation of profound metamorphoses of emotion and spirit within the hero.

Hamlet, for example, not only shows the day to day, minute to minute ebb and flow of Hamlet's mourning, of "that within which passes show," but also the sea change in the apparent resolution of his grief at the end of the play, when he seems to change from the "young Hamlet," an undergraduate, to a man of thirty,[37] when he becomes more conscious that he is "but one," when he acknowledges the special providence in the fall of a sparrow, when his manic talk subsides, when for the first time he seems calm, all passion harmonized, if not yet spent. C. S. Lewis intimates that we cannot explain the enormous change that comes over Hamlet, though we know precisely when it happens.[38] I think we can explain it, however, as long as we see his character, as Lewis himself wishes to, as an expression of the whole action, of what happens to others as well as to himself. For at the end of the play the hectic is in the King's blood, the uncontainable and corrupting anger of grief is Laertes's, some of the sorrow and guilt Gertrude's, and the extreme sorrow of madness and suicide, Ophelia's. Both the small and largest movements of Hamlet's passion, thus, are dramatized not only in what he says, powerful and revealing as his soliloquies and speeches may be, but in what happens to and in others. As in the moralities, the action, though it is now literal as well as partially figurative, is the anatomy of the metamorphosis of his inner life, the continuous pulsations of thought and feeling, outward as well as inward, that finally enable him to proclaim, with confidence and with our understanding, "This is I, / Hamlet the Dane" (5.1.254–55).

Othello similarly dramatizes a phenomenal metamorphosis and recovery in the psychic and spiritual life of its hero, and it too capitalizes on potentialities of morality drama in doing so. The underlying morality schema in *Othello* is relatively simpler and clearer than in *Hamlet*, and its movements of passion, also, must be understood in terms broader than the hero's own speeches and action. The two antagonists for Othello's soul are Desdemona and Iago, who represent not so much allegorical figures of salvation and damnation (though those overtones remain important), as the literalized equivalents within Othello of his faith and of his despair, of his capacity to love his wife as he loves himself and of his failure to do so. The two together—the conflict between them and the movement from one to the other—constitute his character, not just one or the other. Critics of *Othello* tend to employ the epistemology either of Iago or of Desdemona: Shakespeare had the rare capacity to do both. The scene in which Iago successfully tempts Othello (3.3), for example, usually most captures the attention of critics; and its discrimination of the process of Othello's fall into despair, the minute inflections and movements of his thoughts and emotions, is indeed extraordinarily gripping. But the length and fullness of that discrimination shows us Othello's resistance to the demonic social image of himself that Iago shows him as well as his vulnerability to it,[39] and Desdemona's image of him remains a deep part of him even in this scene. Many critics extol Desdemona largely for the purpose of showing Othello's unworthiness of her, but her luminousness is also an image of the luminousness of Othello's love for her. She is most eloquent and forceful at the beginning of the play when his love for her is strong; she speaks bewilderedly and less powerfully, though hardly less movingly, when his love weakens. But the part of him she represents is never absent, which is one of the principal reasons he remains heroic.

Macbeth, which represents the almost literal decomposition of a man, perhaps more than any other of the tragedies most closely discriminates the synapses of the hero's turns of thought and emotion. The play, which is about regression to primitive thinking and feeling, primarily shows us a man "rapt" in thought. Much of this rapture, the "torture of the mind . . . in restless ecstasy" (3.2.23–24), is represented in the remarkable soliloquies that depict not just what, but how, Macbeth thinks—how his thoughts are propelled by his imagination and feelings. Some of the deepest actions of Macbeth's emotional life, however, are represented in what is apparently outside him. The bloody dagger is a hallucination that he describes for us; the dark and bloody kingdom that he creates in his image we see and experience ourselves, and the more absolutely he becomes identified with it—the less distinction there is for him between what is outside and inside himself—the more the inner atrophy of his being is revealed. Equally revealing is his relation with Lady Macbeth. We often quote, and schoolchildren still memorize, Macbeth's soliloquies, but what most sustains the dramatic interest of the play is the marriage that is at once a literal relationship of a man and a woman and a figurative representation of the motions and changes that compose, as Freud suggested, a single psychic entity. When Macbeth and Lady Macbeth are together, we see the murderous conjunction of "frozen conscience and hot burning will" that composes Macbeth's "great passion of fear and fury." As they separate, we see the increasing fragmentation and cauterization of feeling that Lady Macbeth acts out in her somnambulism and suicide but that also transpires within Macbeth. The whole process of their relationship constitutes the representation of a soul in motion.

The tremendous flux of passion in Lear, finally, is less linear than it is in any of the other heroes, but it too is eventually understood and experienced by an audience as much by what is projected outside of him as by what he himself says. His speeches and soliloquies detail the oscillations of love and rage that are the expressions of his denial of death, but those oscillations are also shown in everything and everyone with whom he comes into contact. The distinction between what is outside of Lear and inside of him cannot even be made in the expressionistic storm scene, which may be one reason why the scene is extremely difficult to stage.[40] In other parts of the play the two are more distinguishable, but just as deeply connected. The pain of Gloucester's blinding, the "eyes' anguish" (4.5.6), is a variation on the suffering of Lear's madness, the "eye of anguish" (4.3.15), but it is also a physical image of it. Virtually all of the characters in the play are in a sense Lear's offspring, if not images, felt and understood by us primarily as they relate to, feel about—and often express—him: the daughter and Fool who love him, the daughters who seek to destroy him, the faithful servant who exists for him, the exiled son whose apparent madness and nakedness mimic him, the son-in-law who is moved by him. Lear comes to know himself (as well as to be known by us) in all of these characters, but perhaps most in his actual children, since all three are parts of him, though it is the good one that finally means the most to us as well as to him. Cordelia (and the Fool as a surrogate for her) is always, both in her own simplicity and in the complexity of what she signifies for and about Lear, an expression of the turbulent currents of Lear's own emotions: the stubbornness and its undertow of symbiotic motion between the pride of life and the undeniability of death; the memory of her, embodied in the words and figure of the Fool, that wells up in his heart and drives him mad; the reunion with her that is the prelude to the final combination of joy and sorrow that brings him to rest in death.

The distinction of the four great tragedies is their dramatization of these kinds of fundamentally internal formations and transformations of feeling in human suffering, and we should not take that distinction for granted. Few other works of literature, in the English Renaissance or in any other period, can rival the representation of the tidal currents of the heart and spirit in these oceanic plays. Even Shakespeare's other tragedies do not quite do so. Some obvious interior changes are shown in Romeo, and incipiently deeper ones are revealed in Juliet, but the circumstances that cause their tragedy really are extrinsic to them and are not, as in the major tragedies, an expression of their own natures. Richard III's quest and final confrontation with his conscience suggest only the skeleton of *Macbeth*. Richard II's elegiac grief anticipates the emotional state of Hamlet, as well as of Lear, but it is remarkably static by comparison. Both *Richard III* and *Richard II*, moreover, are as much about the soul of England as they are about the souls of their heroes.

To a considerable extent, the same is true of the Roman tragedies, even the later ones. They are consciously historicist, and in all of them Shakespeare seems at least as interested in how

Roman culture both produces the hero and fails him as he is in
the hero's inner life. Shakespeare presents the Roman heroes as
an inextricable part of a historical tableau, drawn largely by Plutarch, in which individual motivations can be inferred but not
known. Shakespeare makes small changes in Plutarch that can
turn out to be enormous, but they are not usually in the direc-
tion of introspection. There are comparatively few soliloquies in
the plays. There are suggestions of psychological depth in Brutus
and Cassius considered as a composite entity, but separately they
are ultimately overshadowed by Caesar, for whom *Julius Caesar* is
properly named, and his character is almost entirely public and
political. His emotions are largely unknowable. *Coriolanus* and
Antony and Cleopatra are far more psychologically rich, and their
heroes do undergo significant changes, but both Coriolanus and
Antony remain fundamentally defined as heroes by their pursuit
of glory, and this is true even of Antony's erotic investment in
Cleopatra. They are thus depicted mainly, and necessarily, as political figures. In the storm in *King Lear*, Coriolanus, as Bradley
noted, would simply have gritted his teeth, partly because of his
disposition, but partly because his identity *is* so culturally con-
tingent. The tragedy for Coriolanus is precisely that contingency,
but it is a tragedy that limits the depth of what Shakespeare can
show within him. Coriolanus, whose "heart's his mouth"
(3.1.257), certainly speaks what he feels, and his character is am-
plified by being represented in others, Volumnia and Aufidius
especially, but these amplifications, even Volumnia's, as well as
his own speeches, usually have a marked political inflection. Antony's magnanimity and passion for Cleopatra make him far
more accessible to modern taste, but though we witness his many
outward motions, in his characterization, too, those that are
within him are not revealed in depth. As the critical scene with
the soothsayer makes clear (2.3), he is fractured more by historical necessity, the inexorable changes in the Roman Empire, than
by his own nature. (It is interestingly Plutarch, not Shakespeare,
who insists unequivocally upon a psychomachic interpretation
of Antony's actions.) Antony's character is deepened, in the fashion of the four major tragedies, by being reflected, after his death
as well as before, in Cleopatra; and there are suggestive and pow-

erful introspective moments, as when he tells Eros that like a cloud he cannot hold his "visible shape" (4.15.1–22). But what is not visible we only rarely see. We see it even less in Cleopatra, whose nature seems far more independent of politics. She is an endlessly fertile creation, not least in her literally minute to minute changes, but we are not really ever allowed to experience those changes from the inside. In the four major tragedies, ultimately nothing can compete with our attention to the suffering of the hero. In *Coriolanus* and *Antony and Cleopatra*, and *Julius Caesar*, in the manner of the history plays, the state itself does. The protagonists of these dramas, in the last analysis, are creatures as well as victims of Rome, and the plays are at least as much dispassionate tragedies of particular societies that lack the possibility of communion as they are tragedies of individual suffering.

In *Hamlet, Othello, Macbeth*, and *King Lear*, the hero is revealed in a host of cultural manifestations, including, of course, political and social ones, but these manifestations almost all eventually lead inward, and finally it is the interior drama of suffering, what the Renaissance called the perturbations of the mind, the profound movement of fundamental passions, in both their particularity and universality, upon which Shakespeare most concentrates: love, joy, hatred, fear, despair, rage, the ways of grief, of erotic yearning, of self-destruction, of dying. These are experiences that no new philosophy will ever succeed in calling in doubt, and Shakespeare dramatizes them in these tragedies so deeply, with such intensity and such fidelity, that after four centuries the plays seem still to echo the pulses of our own lives.

NOTES

INDEX

NOTES

"FOR HE WAS GREAT OF HEART"

1.   Simon Forman, *The Booke of Plaies and Notes therof per Formans for Common Pollicie*, quoted in the introduction to the New Arden ed. of *Macbeth*, ed. Kenneth Muir (London: Methuen, 1977), pp. xiii–xiv. For an interesting discussion of Forman's accounts of Shakespeare performances, see Don LePan, *The Cognitive Revolution in Western Culture* (London: Macmillan, 1989), pp. 280–302.

2.   Pierre Charron, *Of Wisedome*, trans. Samson Lennard (London: ca. 1606; facsim. ed., New York: Da Capo Press, 1971), sig. F4. Transcriptions of sixteenth- and seventeenth-century texts in this study, whether from early or modern editions, follow modern practice with *i, j, v,* and long *s*.

3.   All references to Shakespeare are to *The Complete Works*, ed. Stanley Wells and Gary Taylor (New York: Oxford Univ. Press, 1986).

4.   Thomas Wright, *The Passions of the Minde in Generall* (London, 1604; facsim. ed., Urbana: Univ. of Illinois Press, 1971), sig. Bv. The introduction to this edition, by Thomas O. Sloan, gives a cogent summary of Renaissance views of the passions.

5.   Pierre de La Primaudaye, *The French Academie* (London, 1586), sig. A2.

6.   Much commentary in Charron's *Of Wisedome*, for example, is paraphrased from Montaigne, without attribution.

7.   For a further discussion of Posthumus's relation to Cloten, see Arthur Kirsch, *Shakespeare and the Experience of Love* (Cambridge: Cambridge Univ. Press, 1981), pp. 153–61.

8.   See Eleanor Prosser, "Shakespeare, Montaigne, and the 'Rarer Action,'" *Shakespeare Studies* 1 (1965): 261–64.

9. A. C. Bradley, *Shakespearean Tragedy* (London: Macmillan, 1905), p. 20.

10. A. P. Rossiter, *Angel with Horns* (New York: Theatre Arts Books, 1961), p. 263.

11. Ibid., p. 264.

12. All references to *King Lear* in this book are to *The Tragedy of King Lear: The Folio Text* in the Oxford *Complete Works.*

13. Quoted in E. K. Chambers, *The Elizabethan Stage*, 4 vols. (Oxford: Clarendon Press, 1961), 2: 309.

14. Bradley, *Shakespearean Tragedy*, pp. 32–33.

15. Lily B. Campbell, *Shakespeare's Tragic Heroes: Slaves of Passion* (Cambridge: Cambridge Univ. Press, 1930).

16. William Empson, *Some Versions of Pastoral* (New York: New Directions, 1960), chap. 2, "Double Plots."

17. Northrop Frye, *Fools of Time* (Toronto: Univ. of Toronto Press, 1967), pp. 3, 4–5, 6.

18. All references to the Bible are to *The Geneva Bible*, a facsimile ed. of the 1560 translation (Madison: Univ. of Wisconsin Press, 1969).

19. A. D. Nuttall, *A New Mimesis: Shakespeare and the Representation of Reality* (London: Methuen, 1983), pp. 166–67.

20. Ibid., pp. 28, 177.

21. Jean Starobinski, "Psychoanalysis and Literary Understanding," *The Living Eye*, trans. Arthur Goldhammer (Cambridge: Harvard Univ. Press, 1989), pp. 146–47.

22. See Kirsch, *Shakespeare and the Experience of Love*, pp. 3–8, for a fuller discussion of the bearing of mysteries as well as the moralities upon the use of Freudian and Christian ideas in interpreting Shakespeare's plays.

23. Samuel Johnson, *Johnson on Shakespeare*, ed. Arthur Sherbo, vols. 7 and 8 of *The Yale Edition of the Works of Samuel Johnson* (New Haven: Yale Univ. Press, 1968), 7:62.

HAMLET

1. Cited in Alan S. Downer, *The British Drama* (New York: Appleton-Century-Crofts, 1950), p. 78.

2. I assume throughout this argument that Shakespeare essentially accepts and draws nourishment from the conventions of the revenge drama and that the ghost represents Hamlet's tragic predicament more than he does a strictly moral issue. Shakespeare clearly sophisticates Kyd's conception by conflating

the ghost of Andrea and the figure of Revenge and by bringing the ghost directly into the world of the play and into Hamlet's consciousness; but there is little question, either by Hamlet or by us, that Hamlet must eventually obey the ghost's injunction to take revenge. In later dramas like *The Atheist's Tragedy* and *The Revenge of Bussy D'Ambois*, the ghosts themselves remind the heroes that revenge belongs to God, but it is hardly an accident that those plays are neither tragic nor particularly compelling. The whole issue of the ethos of revenge in *Hamlet* is discussed most convincingly, it seems to me, by Helen Gardner in *The Business of Criticism* (Oxford: Oxford Univ. Press, 1959), pp. 35–51, and Roland M. Frye, *The Renaissance Hamlet* (Princeton: Princeton Univ. Press, 1984). For a contrary interpretation of the issue, see especially Fredson Bowers, *Elizabethan Revenge Tragedy* (Princeton: Princeton Univ. Press, 1940), and "Hamlet as Minister and Scourge," *PMLA* 70 (1955): 740–49; and Eleanor Prosser, *Hamlet and Revenge* (Stanford: Stanford Univ. Press, 1967).

3. *The Jew of Malta*, ed. N. W. Bawcutt, The Revels Plays (Manchester: Manchester Univ. Press, 1978), 3.2.13–14.

4. *The Spanish Tragedy*, ed. Philip Edwards, The Revels Plays (Cambridge: Harvard Univ. Press, 1959).

5. T. S. Eliot, *Selected Essays* (London: Faber and Faber, 1951), p. 145.

6. Jacques Lacan, "Desire and the Interpretation of Desire in *Hamlet*," *Yale French Studies* 55/56 (1977): 37–39.

7. For a similar view of this issue, see Meredith Skura, *The Literary Use of the Psychoanalytic Process* (New Haven: Yale Univ. Press, 1981), pp. 41–43, 46–53.

8. The definition of incest between a man and his brother's wife in the Elizabethan period was essentially a legal one—the relationship was prohibited by canon and civil law—but Claudius's actual murder of his brother suggests the deeper psychic implications of incest as well.

9. For the most illuminating recent discussion of the literary treatment of melancholy in Renaissance England, see Bridget Gellert Lyons, *Voices of Melancholy* (New York: Barnes and Noble, 1971). Lyons's analysis of Hamlet's melancholy (pp. 77–112) is especially rich, and I found it suggestive for my own argument, though my emphasis and method are different from hers. Campbell discusses the relevance of Elizabethan ideas of grief to *Hamlet* in *Shakespeare's Tragic Heroes*, pp. 109–47, but treats the subject rather as the King does, as a moral infirmity.

10. For a sophisticated discussion of mourning and melancholy in *Hamlet* that appeared at about the same time as my original essay on the play and proceeds on similar lines, see Alexander Welsh, "The Task of Hamlet," *Yale Review* 69 (1980): 481–502. The relevance of modern psychoanalytic ideas of mourning to the play is also touched upon by Paul A. Jorgenson, "Hamlet's Therapy," *Huntington Library Quarterly* 27 (1964): 239–58, and is discussed in more depth,

though in ways that quickly become remote from the play, by Lacan, "Desire and the Interpretation of Desire in *Hamlet*," pp. 11–52.

11. Translated by Joan Rivière, in *Freud: General Psychological Theory*, ed. Philip Rieff (New York: Collier, 1963), p. 165. Unless otherwise noted, all other references to Freud are to James Strachey, trans. and ed., *The Standard Edition of the Complete Psychological Works of Sigmund Freud*, 24 vols. (London: Hogarth Press, 1953–74).

12. Freud, "Mourning and Melancholia," Rivière trans., p. 166.

13. Ibid., pp. 166, 169–70.

14. Ibid., p. 170.

15. C. S. Lewis, "Hamlet: The Prince or the Poem," *Proceedings of the British Academy* 28 (1942): 138–54. G. Wilson Knight also focuses on "the devil of the knowledge of death, which possesses Hamlet" (*The Wheel of Fire* [London: Methuen, 1949], p. 39), but Lewis's discussion is less invidious and much more spacious, not least because it takes account of the dramatic impact of the ghost in the play.

16. See Lyons, *Voices of Melancholy*, p. 81.

17. Roland Frye, *Renaissance Hamlet*, pp. 76–110.

18. Freud, "Mourning and Melancholis," Rivière trans., p. 167.

19. For a full discussion of the traditions of thought that lie behind Hamlet's contemplation of death in this scene, see Roland Frye, *Renaissance Hamlet*, pp. 205–53.

20. Northrop Frye, *Fools of Time*, pp. 38–39.

21. I borrow this formulation, which describes a reversal of the process of identification in depression, from Karl Abraham, who does not himself apply it to Hamlet. In common with many more recent psychoanalytic writers, Abraham argues that an essential part of the resolution of grief consists of the unambivalent and beneficent introjection of the loved person into the mourner's own psyche to compensate for the continuing, conscious sense of loss. See his *Selected Papers* (London: Hogarth Press, 1968), pp. 442, 438.

22. The therapeutic value of this kind of aggressive transference was accentuated and made quite explicit by Marston in *The Malcontent*; see Lyons, *Voices of Melancholy*, pp. 96–97.

23. Freud, "Mourning and Melancholia," Rivière trans., pp. 167–68.

OTHELLO

1. See Rosalie Colie, *Shakespeare's Living Art* (Princeton: Princeton Univ. Press, 1974), pp. 135–67.

2. *The Book of Common Prayer, 1559*, ed. John E. Booty (Charlottesville: Univ. Press of Virginia, 1976), p. 297. The biblical text (Ephesians 5:28–32) varies slightly in the Geneva translation.

3. "The Most Prevalent Form of Degradation in Erotic Life," trans. Joan Rivière, in *Freud: Sexuality and the Psychology of Love*, ed. Philip Rieff (New York: Collier, 1963), pp. 59–61.

4. Rossiter, *Angel with Horns*, p. 206.

5. W. H. Auden, *The Dyer's Hand* (New York: Random House, 1968), pp. 268–69.

6. Richard Marienstras, *New Perspectives on the Shakespearean World* (Cambridge: Cambridge Univ. Press, 1985), p. 131. Marienstras's reading of Othello's "story" is a good tonic against the current deconstructive disposition to stress its "narrativity." Cf. Stephen Greenblatt, *Renaissance Self-Fashioning* (Chicago: Univ. of Chicago Press, 1980), pp. 237–38.

7. Thomas Rymer, "The Tragedies of the Last Age," in *Critical Essays of the Seventeenth Century*, ed. J. E. Spingarn, 3 vols. (London: Oxford Univ. Press, 1908), 2:221.

8. "What is symbolized as a virgin" in romance, Northrop Frye maintains, "is actually a human conviction, however expressed, that there is something at the core of one's infinitely fragile being which is not only immortal but has discovered the secret of invulnerability that eludes the tragic hero" (*The Secular Scripture* [Cambridge: Harvard Univ. Press, 1976], p. 86). Though Desdemona herself is not invulnerable, her love is. Elizabethan theological writers commonly equated virginity with marital chastity. Henry Bullinger, for example, quoted St. John Crysostom: "The first degree of chastity is unspotted virginity; the second is faithful wedlock" (*The Decades of Henry Bullinger*, Parker Society ed., 4 vols. [Cambridge: Cambridge Univ. Press, 1849–52], 1:402).

9. See Ernest Brennecke, " 'Nay, That's Not Next!': The Significance of Desdemona's 'Willow Song,' " *Shakespeare Quarterly* 4 (1953): 35–38.

10. See Lawrence J. Ross, "World and Chrysolite in *Othello*," *Modern Language Notes* 76 (1961): 683–92.

11. See John E. Seaman, "Othello's Pearl," *Shakespeare Quarterly* 19 (1968): 81–85.

12. G. K. Hunter, "Othello and Colour Prejudice," *Dramatic Identities and Cultural Tradition* (Liverpool: Liverpool Univ. Press, 1978), pp. 31–59.

13. Northrop Frye, *Fools of Time*, p. 102.

14. Quoted in Hunter, *Dramatic Identities*, pp. 48–49.

15. For an excellent discussion of the Elizabethan decorum of Othello's public behavior, see John Holloway, *The Story of the Night* (Lincoln: Univ. of Nebraska Press, 1961), pp. 40–42.

16. For discussions of the mixture of comic and tragic expectations in *Othello*, see Thomas McFarland, *Tragic Meanings in Shakespeare* (New York: Random House, 1966), pp. 60–91; Barbara Heliodora C. de Mendonça, " 'Othello': A Tragedy Built on a Comic Structure," *Shakespeare Survey* 21 (1968): 31–38; and Susan Snyder, *The Comic Matrix of Shakespeare's Tragedies* (Princeton: Princeton Univ. Press, 1979), pp. 70–90.

17. Northrop Frye, *Fools of Time*, p. 102; Knight, *Wheel of Fire*, pp. 97–119.

18. See Marienstras's discussion of "the fairy tale perfection" of Desdemona as well as of Othello in *New Perspectives*, pp. 139, and 126–59 passim.

19. Freud, "On Narcissism: An Introduction," *Works*, 14:88, 100; idem, "Femininity," *Works*, 22:133–34.

20. Freud, "Degradation in Erotic Life," Rivière trans., pp. 60–61; idem, "On Narcissism," *Works*, 14:88, 100.

21. See Frederick Goldin, *The Mirror of Narcissus* (Ithaca: Cornell Univ. Press, 1967).

22. Northrop Frye, *A Natural Perspective* (New York: Columbia Univ. Press, 1967), p. 132; idem, *Secular Scripture*, pp. 149, 153.

23. Northrop Frye, *Fools of Time*, p. 5.

24. Knight, *Wheel of Fire*, p. 111.

25. Northrop Frye, *Fools of Time*, p. 5.

26. See especially *Beyond the Pleasure Principle, Works*, 18:49–57.

27. See Stephen Greenblatt's rich discussion of this scene in *Renaissance Self-Fashioning*, pp. 240–44. I think the ambivalence Othello expresses is less a depiction of a "tension" between erotic desire and Christian orthodoxy than a tragic representation of the finiteness of human existence itself. Greenblatt's argument includes both points, but it stresses the former. In *Othello*, it seems to me, the primary quarrel is with the limitations of life, not of doctrine.

28. F. R. Leavis, "Diabolic Intellect and the Noble Hero," *Scrutiny* 6 (1937): 264, 270.

29. Bernard Spivack, *Shakespeare and the Allegory of Evil* (New York: Columbia Univ. Press, 1958), pp. 415–53.

30. Leah Scragg, "Iago—Vice or Devil?" *Shakespeare Survey* 21 (1968): 53–65.

31. Charron, *Of Wisedome*, sig. Mm3v.

32. See Meredith Skura, "Shakespeare's Psychology: Characterization in Shakespeare," in *William Shakespeare: His World, His Work, His Influence*, ed. John Andrews, 3 vols. (New York: Charles Scribner's Sons, 1985), 2:584–85.

33. Edward Snow, "Sexual Anxiety and the Male Order of Things in *Othello*," *English Literary Renaissance* 10 (1980): 384–412, focuses on this issue. The limitation of Snow's often brilliant readings, however, is that the clinical details he

finds in the play's imagery are evidence of the comprehensiveness of Shakespeare's genius, not of its diagnostic purposes.

34. See Northrop Frye, *Fools of Time*, p. 103.

35. Auden, *The Dyer's Hand*, p. 266.

36. Freud, *Works*, 21:144.

37. Freud, "Degradation in Erotic Life," Rivière trans., pp. 62, 65, 68.

38. John Florio, trans. *The Essayes of Montaigne*, 3 vols. (London: Dent, 1927) 3:105, 72, 77, 106, 115, 75.

MACBETH

1. Macbeth's egoism is especially stressed by Helen Gardner, "Milton's 'Satan' and the Theme of Damnation in Elizabethan Tragedy," *Essays & Studies* 1 (1948): 44–66; Rossiter, *Angel with Horns*, pp. 209–34; and Gordon Braden, "Senecan Tragedy and the Renaissance," *Illinois Classical Studies* 9 (1984): 277–92.

2. Mary McCarthy, "General Macbeth," *Harper's Magazine* (June 1962); rpt. in the Signet ed. of *Macbeth*, ed. Sylvan Barnet (New York: New American Library, 1963), p. 232.

3. St. Augustine, book 14, chaps. 13–15, *City of God*, trans. John Healey, ed. R. V. G. Tasker (London: Dent, 1945) 2:43–46.

4. For discussions of the parallels between the two works, see M. C. Bradbrook, "The Sources of *Macbeth*," *Shakespeare Survey* 4 (1951): 35–48; Kenneth Muir, ed., *Macbeth*, New Arden ed. (Cambridge: Harvard Univ. Press, 1977), pp. 189–90; and Ian Donaldson, *The Rapes of Lucretia* (Oxford: Clarendon Press, 1982), pp. 51–52.

5. For illuminating discussions of the self-destructive nature of Tarquin's rape of Lucrece, see Sam Hynes, "The Rape of Tarquin," *Shakespeare Quarterly* 10 (1959): 451–53; and Donaldson, *Rapes of Lucretia*, p. 52.

6. Freud, "Those Wrecked by Success," *Works*, 14:324.

7. Muir focuses on this speech in his introduction to the New Arden ed. of *Macbeth*, pp. xxiii–xxix.

8. See Glynne Wickham, "Hell Gate and Its Door-Keeper," *Shakespeare Survey* 19 (1966): 68–74.

9. La Primaudaye, *The French Academie*, sig. [P8].

10. Ibid., sig. Q3v.

11. The phrase is from the third part of the "Homily against disobedience and wilfull Rebellion": "Where most rebellions and rebelles bee, there is the

expresse similitude of hell, and the rebelles themselves are the verie figures of fiendes and devils" (*Certaine Sermons or Homilies appointed to be Read in Churches in the Time of Queen Elizabeth I* [1623; facsim., ed. Mary Rickey and Thomas B. Stroup, Gainesville: Scholars' Facsimiles & Reprints, 1968]), p. 296.

12. Freud, *Works*, 14:321.

13. For a general discussion of the issue of parricide, see Northrop Frye, *Fools of Time*, pp. 3–39. Norman Rabkin, *Shakespeare and the Problem of Meaning* (Chicago: Univ. of Chicago Press, 1981), pp. 101–10, has a suggestive discussion of parricidal motifs in *Macbeth*. Rabkin sees parricide as an alternative to ambition in explaining Macbeth's motives; my own interest is in understanding parricide as a deep expression of Macbeth's ambition. In an argument that appeared at the same time as my initial article on *Macbeth*, Robert N. Watson, *Shakespeare and the Hazards of Ambition* (Cambridge: Harvard Univ. Press, 1984), pp. 83–141, takes such a view as well, though my emphasis, unlike his, is on narcissism.

14. *The Confessions of the Incomparable Doctour S. Augustine* (London, 1620), sig. Bv.

15. Montaigne, *Essayes*, 1:104–5.

16. Cf. Harry Berger, "The Early Scenes of *Macbeth*: Preface to New Interpretation," *ELH* 47 (1980): 1–31. Berger's readings of the opening scene are fertile and valuable, but I think his consequent "challenge" to the "orthodox view" of the play depends upon an over-simplified construction of that view to begin with.

17. Freud, "Criminals from a Sense of Guilt," *Works*, 14:332–33.

18. Samuel Taylor Coleridge, *Shakespearean Criticism*, 2 vols., ed. Thomas Raysor (London: Dent, 1960), 1:64. References to *Paradise Lost* are to the text in *The Poems of John Milton*, ed. John Carey and Alastair Fowler (London: Longmans, 1968).

19. *Confessions of the Incomparable Doctour Augustine*, sig. Bv.

20. Freud, "Animism, Magic, and the Omnipotence of Thoughts," *Works*, 13:85.

21. Ibid., p. 91.

22. Ibid., pp. 91, 85.

23. Ibid., p. 86.

24. Rossiter, *Angel with Horns*, p. 218.

25. See Michael Goldman's fine discussion of the play in *Acting and Action in Shakespearean Tragedy* (Princeton: Princeton Univ. Press, 1985), pp. 94–111.

26. Charron, *Of Wisedome*, sigs. H2–H2v.

27. Muir, ed., *Macbeth* (introduction, pp. xxvii–xxix) calls attention to reiterated images of separation and disjunction in the play. He does not pursue their

psychological implications. Interestingly, in *Doctor Faustus*, Marlowe's exploration of necromantic thinking, images of bodily separation are acted out.

28. Cited by Muir, ed., *Macbeth*, p. 50n.

29. Montaigne, *Essayes*, 2:326–27.

30. Wallace Stevens, *Opus Posthumous*, ed. Samuel French Morse (New York: Knopf, 1957), p. 163.

31. Freud, *Works*, 14:324.

32. For the classic discussion of the imagery of infants in the play, see Cleanth Brooks, "The Naked Babe and the Cloak of Manliness," *The Well Wrought Urn* (New York: Harcourt, Brace & World, 1947).

33. For a different and important reading of this phrase, see Janet Adelman, "'Born of Woman': Fantasies of Maternal Power in *Macbeth*," in *Cannibals, Witches, and Divorce*, ed. Marjorie Garber (Baltimore: Johns Hopkins Univ. Press, 1987), who argues that "the whole of the play represents in very powerful form both the fantasy of virtually absolute and destructive maternal power and the fantasy of absolute escape from the power" (p. 90).

34. Berger, "The Early Scenes of *Macbeth*," p. 4. For a more comprehensive argument for the indeterminacy of *Macbeth*, see Stephen Booth, *King Lear, Macbeth, Indefinition, and Tragedy* (New Haven: Yale Univ. Press, 1983), pp. 81–118.

35. See Adelman, "'Born of Woman,'" pp. 107–9, for a more censorious reading of Macduff, which takes issue with mine. I think it is plausible to argue that Macduff left Lady Macduff and his family without telling them precisely to protect them, from the charge of treason. The first question the murderer asks is, "Where is your husband?" and then calls him a "traitor" (4.2.81, 84), the word upon which Lady Macduff and her son have been playing throughout the scene.

KING LEAR

1. See especially Holloway, *Story of the Night*, pp. 85–91. For a suggestive survey of biblical echoes in the play, which includes but does not give particular emphasis to Ecclesiastes, see Rosalie L. Colie, "The Energies of Endurance: Biblical Echo in *King Lear*," in *Some Facets of King Lear*, ed. Rosalie L. Colie and F. T. Flahiff (Toronto: Univ. of Toronto Press, 1974), pp. 117–44.

2. See McFarland, *Tragic Meanings in Shakespeare*, pp. 149–71.

3. See Holloway, *Story of the Night*, pp. 75–80, and Joseph Wittreich, "*Image of That Horror*": History, Prophecy, and Apocalypse in King Lear (San Marino: Huntington Library Press, 1984).

4. Allan Bloom comments on this speech in his fine essay on *Richard II* in

Shakespeare as Political Thinker, ed. John Alvis and Thomas G. West (Durham: Carolina Academic Press, 1981), pp. 55–56.

5. Enid Welsford, *The Fool* (Garden City, N.Y.: Anchor Books, 1961), pp. 269–70.

6. For thorough discussions of these commentaries, see William Elton, *King Lear and the Gods* (San Marino: Huntington Library Press, 1968), pp. 270–72.

7. Cited in Kenneth Muir, ed., *King Lear,* New Arden ed. (Cambridge: Harvard Univ. Press, 1959), p. 45n. For a discussion of the ballad, see Hyder Rollins, "'King Lear' and the Ballad of 'John Careless,'" *Modern Language Review* 15 (1920): 87–89.

8. See J. V. Cunningham, *Tradition and Poetic Structure* (Denver: Alan Swallow, 1960), pp. 135–41. Cf. Elton, *King Lear and the Gods,* pp. 99–107.

9. See Elton, *King Lear and the Gods,* pp. 249–53.

10. For the argument that Lear's suffering and madness are purgatorial, see Paul A. Jorgenson, *Lear's Self-Discovery* (Berkeley and Los Angeles: Univ. of California Press, 1967).

11. See Knight, "*King Lear* and the Comedy of the Grotesque," *Wheel of Fire,* pp. 160–76.

12. Barbara Everett, "The New *King Lear,*" *Critical Quarterly* 2 (1960): 334–35.

13. See especially "Of the Affection of Fathers to Their Children." Montaigne's assumption is that fathers not only often have to give up power to their children, but should do so.

14. *Johnson on Shakespeare,* 8:704.

15. See Maynard Mack, *King Lear in Our Time* (Berkeley and Los Angeles: Univ. of California Press, 1965), pp. 3–25.

16. In the longer term, in the chronicles, Cordelia commits suicide after Lear's own death. Shakespeare's stress, of course, is on Lear's experience of Cordelia's death.

17. The ground-breaking study on this subject is Susan Snyder's "*King Lear* and the Psychology of Dying," *Shakespeare Quarterly* 33 (1982): 449–60. My own analysis places more emphasis upon Freud's insight into the play, but I remain much indebted to her article.

18. Freud, *Works,* 12:301.

19. Ibid., p. 295.

20. Montaigne, *Essayes,* 2:326–27.

21. Granville Barker, *Prefaces to Shakespeare,* 2 vols. (Princeton: Princeton Univ. Press, 1952), 1:305.

22. I think this is the phenomenon Stanley Cavell is really touching upon in

NOTES

"The Avoidance of Love," *Must We Mean What We Say?* (Cambridge: Cambridge Univ. Press, 1976), pp. 272–300, for in *King Lear* the avoidance of love (as well as the embrace of it) is fundamentally the avoidance of death.

23. Freud, *Works*, 12:299.

24. For an interesting, if highly inferential, insistence on the political motives of the opening scene of *Lear*, see Harry V. Jaffa, "The Limits of Politics: *King Lear*, Act I, scene i," in *Shakespeare's Politics*, pp. 113–38.

25. See Molly Mahood, *Shakespeare's Wordplay* (London: Methuen, 1957), p. 87.

26. See Ernst Kantorowicz, *The King's Two Bodies* (Princeton: Princeton Univ. Press, 1957), pp. 24–41.

27. Freud, *Works*, 12:301.

28. *The History of King Leir 1605* (Oxford: Malone Society, 1907).

29. For a discussion of the generic expectations of romance in *King Lear*, see Leo Salingar, "Romance in *King Lear*," *English* 27 (1978): 5–22.

30. There are redemptive expectations of the morality play in *Lear* that are analogous to the expectations of romance. See Edgar Schell, *Strangers and Pilgrims: From The Castle of Perseverance to King Lear* (Chicago: Univ. of Chicago Press, 1983).

31. See Knight, *Wheel of Fire*, pp. 160–76; and Snyder, *Comic Matrix of Shakespeare's Tragedies*, pp. 137–79.

32. Cf. Thomas P. Roche, Jr., "Nothing Almost Sees Miracles": Tragic Knowledge in *King Lear*," in *On King Lear*, ed. Lawrence Danson (Princeton: Princeton Univ. Press, 1981). pp. 136–62.

33. Bradley, *Shakespearean Tragedy*, p. 291.

34. Ian Kirby, "The Passing of King Lear," *Shakespeare Survey* 41 (1989), pp. 155–57.

35. Northrop Frye, *Fools of Time*, p. 115.

SHAKESPEARE'S HUMANISM

1. Jonathan Dollimore, *Radical Tragedy: Religion, Ideology and Power in the Drama of Shakespeare and His Contemporaries* (Chicago: Univ. of Chicago Press, 1984), p. 157 and passim. For an even more radical Marxist reading of Shakespearian tragedy, which takes Dollimore and others to task for simply inverting Tillyard's Elizabethan worldview without considering Shakespeare's proleptic utopian vision, see Kernan Ryan, *Shakespeare* (Atlantic Highlands, N.J.: Humanities Press, 1989), pp. 44–73 and passim.

2. Greenblatt, *Renaissance Self-Fashioning*, p. 256.

3.   See Stephen Greenblatt, *Shakespearean Negotiations* (Berkeley and Los Angeles: Univ. of California Press, 1988), chap. 1.

4.   See especially Edward Pechter, "New Historicism and Its Discontents: Politicizing Renaissance Drama," *PMLA* 102 (1987): 292–303; William Kerrigan, "Individualism, Historicism, and New Styles of Overreaching," *Philosophy and Literature* 13 (1989): 115–26; and Richard Levin, "Unthinkable Thoughts in the New Historicizing of English Renaissance Drama," *New Literary History*, forthcoming 1990. See also the discussion of Burckhardt in William Kerrigan and Gordon Braden, *The Idea of the Renaissance* (Baltimore: Johns Hopkins Univ. Press, 1989), pp. 3–69.

5.   Cf. Dollimore, *Radical Tragedy*, pp. 73–75.

6.   Sir Philip Sidney, "The Defence of Poesie," in *Elizabethan Critical Essays*, ed. G. Gregory Smith, 2 vols. (London: Oxford Univ. Press, 1950), 1:156, and 150–207 passim.

7.   Nuttall, *A New Mimesis*, p. 75.

8.   Sidney, "Defence," p. 164.

9.   The phrase is Richard Levin's "Unthinkable Thoughts" (n. 4 above).

10.   Thomas Dekker, *If It Be Not Good* (London, 1612), prologue.

11.   See Ryan, *Shakespeare*, pp. 58–65.

12.   See Elton, *King Lear and the Gods*; Greenblatt, "Shakespeare and the Exorcists," *Shakespearean Negotiations*; and Ryan, *Shakespeare*, pp. 66–73.

13.   Greenblatt, *Renaissance Self-Fashioning*, pp. 232–54, and Ryan, *Shakespeare*, pp. 51–58.

14.   *Johnson on Shakespeare*, 7:61–62.

15.   See G. F. Parker, *Johnson's Shakespeare* (Oxford: Clarendon Press, 1989), pp. 15–62.

16.   Nuttall, *A New Mimesis*, pp. 99–120.

17.   *Johnson on Shakespeare*, 7:65–66.

18.   *Aristotle on the Art of Poetry*, trans. Lane Cooper (Ithaca: Cornell Univ. Press, 1947), pp. 31–32.

19.   Stephen Greenblatt, "Psychoanalysis and Renaissance Culture," *Literary Theory / Renaissance Texts*, ed. Patricia Parker and David Quint (Baltimore: Johns Hopkins Univ. Press, 1986), pp. 213–15.

20.   Montaigne, *Essayes*, 1:114, 2:323, quoted in *Radical Tragedy*, pp. 17, 39–40.

21.   Montaigne, "Of Experience," *Essayes*, 3:374.

22.   Ibid., 1:141.

23.   Ibid., 3:376.

24. Ibid., p. 23.

25. Ibid., p. 331.

26. Ibid., p. 30.

27. Ibid., pp. 23–24.

28. Ibid., pp. 335–36.

29. Ibid., 2:348, 350.

31. Jean Starobinski, *Montaigne in Motion*, trans. Arthur Goldhammer (Chicago: Univ. of Chicago Press, 1985), p. 307.

32. Freud, *Works*, 14:75.

33. See Thomas McFarland, *Tragic Meanings in Shakespeare*, pp. 149–50, 156.

34. Kirsch, *Shakespeare and the Experience of Love*, pp. 121–27.

35. See Prosser, "Shakespeare, Montaigne, and the 'Rarer Action.'"

36. For a penetrating discussion of the Stoic background of Montaigne's thought, see Gordon Braden, *Renaissance Tragedy and the Senecan Tradition* (New Haven: Yale Univ. Press, 1985, pp. 77–80, 94–98.

37. For a brilliant discussion of Hamlet's growth in terms of Elizabethan categories of age, see Barbara Everett, *Young Hamlet: Essays on Shakespeare's Tragedies* (Oxford: Clarendon Press, 1989), pp. 11–34.

38. Lewis, "Hamlet: The Prince or the Poem," p. 149.

39. Holloway, *Story of the Night*, pp. 155–65, stresses the protracted stage time of Othello's fall.

40. Even Granville Barker had trouble staging these scenes in his production of the play. See Christine Dymkowski, *Harley Granville Barker: A Preface to Modern Shakespeare* (Washington, London, and Toronto: Associated Univ. Presses, 1986), pp. 180–90.

INDEX